AN INTRODUCTION
TO THE ARCHITECTURAL
HERITAGE *of*

SOUTH TIPPERARY

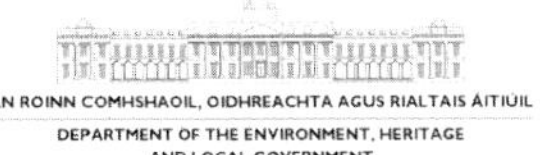

AN ROINN COMHSHAOIL, OIDHREACHTA AGUS RIALTAIS ÁITIUIL
DEPARTMENT OF THE ENVIRONMENT, HERITAGE
AND LOCAL GOVERNMENT

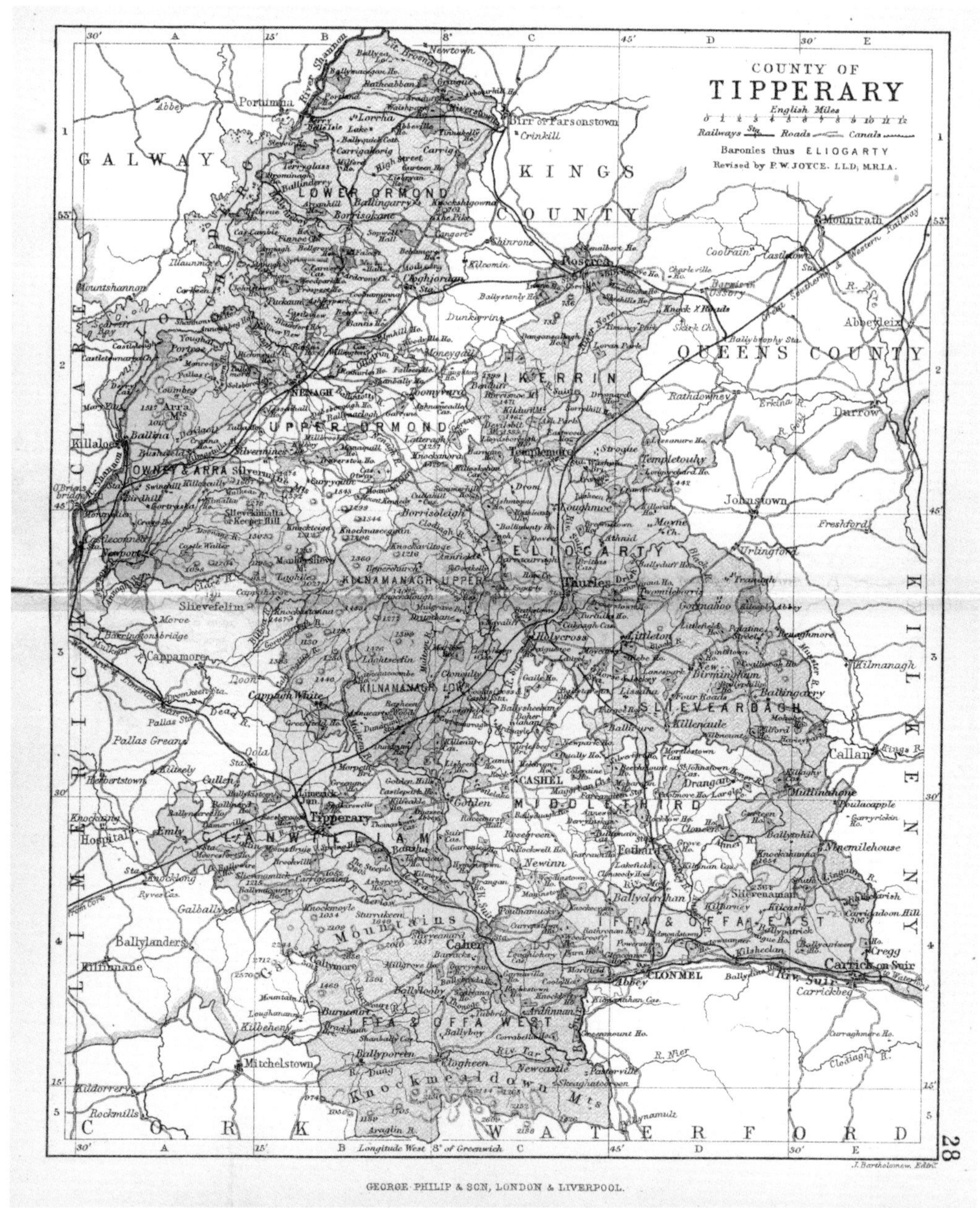

COUNTY OF TIPPERARY
George Philip and Son, London and Liverpool (c. 1885)

This map highlights the various baronies in the historic county of Tipperary. Slieveardagh, Middlethird, Clanwilliam, Iffa and Offa East, Iffa and Offa West, and the parishes of Doon and Toem in Kilnamanagh Upper, all comprise the administrative county of South Tipperary.

Foreword

SLIEVENAMON

A rich folklore says that the mythical warrior Fionn Mac Cumhaill and five companions spent a year in the cairn on the summit engaging in otherworld battles. On another occasion, Fionn climbed the mountain, saying that he would choose as his wife the first maiden to reach the summit the next morning. He smuggled his favourite with him during the night and so the next morning the earliest climber discovered she had already been beaten to the prize. Well-known songs about the mountain include Slievenamon, and The Irish Peasant Girl, composed by local patriot and writer, Charles J. Kickham, and the older traditional Irish Sliabh na mBan.

The Architectural Inventory of South Tipperary was carried out in the summer of 2005. It consists of records of 1,314 buildings and other items within the county that were deemed worthy of recording, of which some 1,251 are being recommended for protection. The Inventory should not be regarded as exhaustive as, over time, other buildings and structures of merit may come to light. The purpose of the Inventory and of this Introduction is to explore the social and historical context of the buildings and to facilitate a greater appreciation of the built heritage of South Tipperary.

The NIAH survey of the architectural heritage of South Tipperary can be accessed on the Internet at: *www.buildingsofireland.ie*

Introduction

The historic county of Tipperary is the largest inland county in Ireland, bordering nine others and extending from the River Shannon and Lough Derg in the north almost to the Waterford estuary in the south. Until the Grand Jury Consolidation Act of 1836, Clonmel was the county town. It had been deemed for some time that Clonmel's location, at the southern extremity of the county, would lead to logistical problems in the administration and governance of the entire county. The Act allowed for the provision of a second assize town, for the northern half of the county, and two years later, under the Local Government Act, the county was divided into two Ridings or distinct functional areas, the two assize towns becoming the county towns for their respective halves of the county. The establishment of county councils in 1899 maintained that division. In 2000, the titles Tipperary (North Riding) and Tipperary (South Riding) were abolished and replaced by North Tipperary and South Tipperary. The seemingly arbitrary dividing line we see today between the administrative counties is based largely on the ancient system of baronies. The parishes of Doon and Toem in Kilnamanagh Upper, and the baronies of Slieveardagh, Middlethird, Clanwilliam, Iffa and Offa East and Iffa and Offa West, form South Tipperary. These last two baronies are the most southerly and bring part of the county into the ancient tribal territory of the Déisí and into the Diocese of Waterford and Lismore. Along with North Tipperary, the adjoining counties are Kilkenny, Waterford, Cork and Limerick.

South Tipperary is defined geographically by the high mountain ranges that enclose its broad, fertile valleys and by the rivers that form part of its boundaries. To the south, the Comeragh and Knockmealdown Mountains form a near continuous barrier, traversed by only a few roads. In the west, the Galtees, Slievenamuck and the Hollyford Hills terminate the level plains. In the south-east of the county, Slievenamon rises as a single-peak landmark above the surrounding countryside, while the Slieveardagh Hills in the north-east of the county are lower, but cover a significant area of land. Less favourable land is generally found around the higher ground, and an outshot of the Bog of Allen extends into the north from Gortnahoe to Ballinure.

Between these mountain ranges, the lower-lying lands, known as the Golden Vale and the Great Plain of Cashel respectively, are drained by the River Suir and its many tributaries: the Multeen, Ara, Aherlow, Tar, Duag, Anner, Lingaun, Clashawley, Moyle and Clodiagh. The Suir is the backbone of the county, providing the focal point for centuries of human settlement. Of the five main centres of population, three are situated directly on the Suir, while four major monastic establishments are to be found on its banks.

The River Suir bisects the county, running north-south through the beautiful Suir valley from Cahir to Newcastle, lying between the Knockmealdowns and the Comeraghs. In this area, still a Gaeltacht up to fifty years ago, the river turns sharply northwards after its confluence with the Nire and forms the boundary with County Waterford as it flows eastwards to join the Nore and the Barrow at the head of Waterford Harbour.

The Suir is tidal up to a few miles beyond Carrick-on-Suir and is navigable as far as Clonmel. This was the great trade route into the heart of South Tipperary and all of east Munster from earliest times, the route of invader and trader, of agricultural and industrial imports and exports, down to the beginning of the twentieth century. But if the Suir was the lifeblood of the region, it also acted as a formidable physical barrier between the east and west of the county. Even today, only nine bridges cross the river between Newcastle and Holycross, some spaced up to 12 km apart ***(fig. 1)***.

The eastern boundary with Kilkenny is defined by the Munster and the King's rivers, both of which are tributaries of the Nore, and by the Lingaun, which flows past the Ahenny slate quarries on its way down to the Suir.

Between the uplands, which are mainly outcrops of Old Red Sandstone, lie the broad valleys, underlain by carboniferous limestone, well drained and forming some of the richest

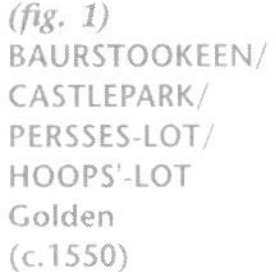

(fig. 1)
BAURSTOOKEEN/
CASTLEPARK/
PERSSES-LOT/
HOOPS'-LOT
Golden
(c.1550)

The bridge at Golden is a long, winding medieval structure with a sixteenth-century tower house of circular plan defending this important crossing of the Suir.

(fig. 2)
CORMAC'S CHAPEL
St Patrick's Rock,
Cashel
(1127-34)

Cormac's Chapel, on the world-famous Rock of Cashel, is undoubtedly Ireland's finest Romanesque building. The north doorway of the chapel displays classic Romanesque lozenge and chevron details. The capitals are, characteristically, all carved differently. The tympanum depicts a scene with a large lion being hunted by a centaur (half-man, half-horse).

(fig. 3)
DERRYNAFLAN ISLAND
Lurgoe
(Monastery founded
sixth century AD)

This monastery, founded by St Ruadhán of Lorrha, is famous for the hoard of eighth and ninth-century ecclesiastical metalwork found here in 1980. It is also said to be the burial place of the mythical master builder, An Gobán Saor. The ruins are of those of a thirteenth-century abbey.

farmland in Ireland. This central plain, traditionally hunting and horse-breeding country, has become a major national and international centre of the bloodstock industry.

The land surface of Ireland has been subjected to great change since prehistory. South Tipperary very strongly bears the imprint of the many layers of change. These changes are still visible in its landscapes, but significant continuity is also found in ancient road alignments, townland boundaries and, most visibly, in the rich legacy of buildings, particularly from the medieval period to the present day.

The earliest evidence for human settlement in South Tipperary, although sparse, dates from Mesolithic times (c. 7000BC to 4000BC). Microliths (tiny flint implements) from this period were found in the 1980s at Ballybrada, near Cahir, on a cliff along the Suir. Stone axeheads from the Neolithic period (c. 4000-2000BC) have also been found in the county, and there is a passage tomb of this era at Shrough, overlooking the Glen of Aherlow in the west and a second possible example on the summit of Slievenamon in the east. Longstone Cullen, near Emly, is a multi-period prehistoric monument comprising a standing stone atop a mound, the latter also containing several barrows or burial mounds. Evidence of Bronze Age metal-working was found at Innyard Hill, near Fethard, and the work of Iron Age goldsmiths at the Golden Bog of Cullen to the west of Tipperary Town. Cahir and Cashel were important settlements early in the first millennium. The destruction of the fort at Cahir in the third century AD is recorded and Cashel was established as a royal site in the following century.

The Rock of Cashel, an iconic place in the national consciousness, represents an even longer connecting thread. Originally the royal seat of the kings of Munster, it went on to become the ecclesiastical capital of the province when Muircheartach Ua Briain donated the site to the church. Cormac's chapel (1127-1134), with its outstanding Hiberno-Romanesque sculpture and wall paintings, represents the high point of the Irish Romanesque ***(fig. 2)***. The complex was abandoned in the eighteenth century for a new cathedral in the town of Cashel. It has since emerged as the internationally renowned site that it is today.

Of the other Early Christian sites, the best known are Ahenny and Toureen Peacaun, because of the richness of their surviving remains. The high crosses of Ahenny form a sub-group with those of nearby Killamery and Kilkieran, both in County Kilkenny. At Toureen, there is a twelfth-century church, a large earthen enclosure, and a collection of incised slabs. At Emly, part of the line of the ancient enclosure surrounding St Ailbe's sixth-century monastery is visible but, apart from a holy well and some carved stone (probably from the ancient cathedral), nothing remains upstanding from this former diocesan centre. The site did not long survive the integration of the diocese of Emly with that of Cashel. The monastery of Derrynaflan ***(fig. 3)***, famous for the hoard of ecclesiastical objects found on this bog island in 1980, is one of a string of early religious sites on the border of Munster and Leinster.

Due to the proximity of the important tenth-century Viking settlement at Waterford, it is likely that Scandinavian settlers explored along the navigable Suir into the heart of Tipperary, although no sites are currently known.

In 1147, a Cistercian foundation was established at present-day Marlfield, just west of Clonmel. The monks had a genius for site selection and chose a river-meadow at Inishlounaght for this, one of the first daughter-houses of Ireland's earliest Cistercian abbey, Mellifont. In 1184 a second abbey was built at Kilcooly, near Urlingford; interestingly, it was constructed under the patronage of Domhnall Mór Ua Briain, despite the arrival of the Normans in the previous decade. Only fragments of the Inishlounaght site survive but these provide a thread of continuity, reused as they were in the nineteenth-century church, on or close to the site of the abbey ***(see fig. 149)***. Kilcooly Abbey, on the other hand, survives as a very complete ruin, cheek by jowl with a fine country house. Hore Abbey (1272), built close to the Rock of Cashel, was the latest of the Cistercian foundations in Ireland.

The most extensive abbey of this period in the whole of Ireland is Athassel Abbey ***(fig. 4)***, a great Augustinian priory founded by William de Burgo sometime before 1200, near Golden, at a crossing-point on the Suir, which was defended with an earthen motte castle. The Augustinian Canons were an integral part of the Norman conquest and their houses were widely dispersed in County Tipperary and in other places where the Normans ventured. One of the factors that made this particular order attractive to powerful patrons like de Burgo was that, unlike other orders such as the Cistercians, the Augustinians were canonically able to receive gifts of church livings and tithes as well as the more familiar endowments of land and property. In this way, foundations like Athassel assisted in the colonial expansion of the Anglo-Normans across the island. In the south, also on the banks of the Suir, is Molough Abbey, the remains of an Augustinian nunnery founded in the fourteenth century by the Butlers.

The late twelfth and thirteenth centuries were a time of great change, with the Anglo-Normans establishing themselves and founding manors, abbeys and towns. Much of Tipperary is an Anglo-Norman creation and the organization that they imposed has lasted into our own time. The distribution map of their settlement shows not only a great density in South Tipperary but also the greatest variety of site types: mottes, moated sites and rectangular enclosures. It also indicates a strong network of market towns and rural villages; most of the former are still going strong, but many of the latter only survive as earthworks in farmland. This density is repeated for tower houses three centuries later ***(fig. 5)***.

(fig. 4)
ATHASSEL ABBEY
Athasselabbey North
(founded c. 1200)

William de Burgo was the patron of this Augustinian priory near Golden, the largest monastic complex in Ireland. Sited on a bank of the River Suir, the evocative ruins comprise a large abbey church, cloister and associated buildings, and the earthwork remains of a contemporary town. All of this is located within a walled precinct protected by a gatehouse and reached by a medieval bridge spanning a former branch of the river which formed an island.

(fig. 5)
LISRONAGH
(medieval)

The present settlement lies at the centre of a very extensive medieval borough. The water in the foreground marks the fosse around an earthen ringwork castle, predecessor of the stone tower house in the background, and the roofless Church of Ireland church is on the site of the medieval parish church. Extensive earthworks in the vicinity indicate the traces of the houses and routeways of the ancient village.

Pre 1700

Over a period of about twenty years, from 1185, the Gaelic order in Tipperary had been disrupted and replaced by a feudal Anglo-Norman regime. Little is known of the detail of this transition. King John established the castle at Ardfinnan in the course of his expedition of 1185. Sometime between then and 1189 he granted land to William de Burgo and Philip of Worcester. These two men, together with Theobald Walter, spearheaded the Anglo-Norman advance, although the Irish chieftains Donal McCarthy of Desmond and Domhnall Mór Ua Briain of Thomond provided steadfast resistance for a time. The annals of the time record the occasional Irish victory but also the relentless progress of Anglo-Norman castle-building, early thirteenth-century examples of which still stand at Cahir ***(fig. 6)***, Carrick, Castlegrace (near Clogheen) and at Kiltinan (near Fethard) ***(see figs. 22-3)***. These acted as centres of colonial control over the newly acquired territories in South Tipperary. By the time of de Burgo's death in 1205 he had consolidated his holdings, sometimes at the expense of his fellow Normans, and was the effective founder of the town of Clonmel, the tithes of the town being attached to Athassel. More significantly, he and his fellow conquerors had put in place a new type of organisation, dividing large tracts of territory into manorial units. These capital manors controlled all land (except church land) within the unit. The Normans used old tribal boundaries as the basis for their subdivisions - into manors for secular purposes and into parishes for religious ones. Within the manor, the lord would make provision for his own demesne and reward his followers with estates. The Normans placed as much importance on agricultural development as they did on organisation so it is not surprising that manorial development was concentrated on the most fertile lands. In addition, they created new monastic foundations and established boroughs and towns in a comprehensive matrix of settlement and governance.

(fig. 6)
CAHIR CASTLE
Castle Street,
Cahir
(early 13th century onwards)

Cahir Castle, one of the most intact medieval fortresses in Ireland, was established in the thirteenth century on the site of an earlier stone fortress, Cathair Dhún Iascaigh, situated on a rocky outcrop over the River Suir. The large keep and part of the great hall to the north-west are thirteenth century and the remaining buildings and structures appear to have been erected by the Butlers in the fifteenth and sixteenth centuries. William Tinsley carried out substantial works in the 1840s.

(fig. 7)
WATERGATE STREET
Fethard
(c. 1600)

The surviving medieval town houses in Fethard are arranged around three sides of the medieval churchyard and, unusually, have their principal entrances at first floor level in their rear wall, facing the church.

(fig. 8)
KILLENURE CASTLE
Killenure
(Early seventeenth century)

Wealthier landowners built substantial houses, known today as fortified houses. The county has many such dwellings, some ruinous and others which were added to in later centuries to become country houses. Killenure, near Dundrum, was the birthplace and family home of Austin Cooper (1759-1830) who in the period 1781 to 1793 recorded and illustrated hundreds of monuments throughout Ireland.

(fig. 9)
FETHARD TOWN HALL
Main Street,Fethard
(c. 1600)

On Fethard's main street, beside the entrance lane to the medieval parish church, stands one of Ireland's oldest civic buildings in continuous use. It began life as an almshouse, part of the structure taking on the functions of the Corporation of Fethard in 1608. It was radically altered c. 1747 and again c. 1840, but the surviving late sixteenth and early seventeenth-century windows, doorways (at the rear) and the ornate chimneystacks all testify to the building's ancient origins.

The number of boroughs established in Tipperary is uncertain, at least thirty-five having been created in the early settlement period. They varied greatly in character: many were effectively farming communities holding land under the burgage system, which meant that they were free from feudal obligations, while other boroughs were substantial centres of population, some of which would be become major urban centres. The medieval town always incorporated a market place and a church, and at least some other familiar features of towns, such as defensive walls, castle, bridge, religious foundation, hospital, school and administration building. And of course the land within the town was further divided into plots set out along streets. Fethard retains several late-sixteenth/early seventeenth-century houses, unusual for having their main entrance doorway in their rear elevations, at first floor level ***(fig. 7)***. The settlement pattern of South Tipperary, today dominated by the towns of Clonmel, Carrick-on-Suir, Tipperary, Cashel, Cahir and Fethard, reflects this Anglo-Norman urban structure created over 700 years ago.

From the fourteenth century onwards, the Butlers and their circumstances were to dominate the county. In the following century, the various branches of the family benefited from the dissolution of the monasteries and notably expanded their landholdings, along with other strong Old English families, such as the Everards, Tobins, Prendergasts and Keatings. In 1328, James Butler was created Earl of Ormond by Edward II and was granted the Liberty of Tipperary, later to be termed the Palatinate of Tipperary. This political entity survived until 1716. The effect was to extend the Butler lordship over the entire county and to establish a quasi-kingdom within a kingdom under the Earl's governance. Palatinate status meant that royal officials were excluded, and that the Earl held his own courts, subject to certain exclusions. The Butlers conducted their rule of the Palatinate in parallel with that of their own estates, which was wise, as governance of the Palatinate could be, and was on occasion, withdrawn by royal decision. The effect of the Palatinate in later times, when the influence of the crown had diminished, meant that the population had greater stability of government than had their counterparts in neighbouring counties.

South Tipperary has one of the densest concentrations of tower houses in Ireland, some 175 definite or likely examples being known. These structures, most of which are four or five-storey stone-built structures, represent the lightly fortified dwellings of higher status citizens. The first half of the seventeenth century saw the construction of the earliest examples of the 'Big House', dwellings which show little or no sign of defensive features and which display large windows ***(fig. 8)***.

In Fethard, a charter issued in 1608 by James I allowed for the building 'in some convenient place [of] a Common Hall or Tollsill [tholsel]... to deliberate and consult touching the publick Welfare'. This tholsel or town hall appears to have been incorporated into the almshouse building on Main Street, built c.1600, and known as Fethard Town Hall ***(fig. 9)***. It is one of Ireland's oldest civic buildings, having been in local authority ownership since the charter of 1608 and still retains obvious features of an early date, such as octagonal-profile cut-limestone chimneys, two Tudor-arched doorways in the rear wall, and several small windows with hood-mouldings. The front façade has three seventeenth-century plaques, one a crucifixion plaque relating to the use of the building as an almshouse, the others being armorial plaques of the Everards, proprietors of the town, and of the Dunboynes, their overloads based at Kiltinan.

One of the strongest characteristics of the landscape of Tipperary is that it is a product of successive modifications of long-established settlement and ownership patterns. The influence of the Butlers had ensured that, in the upheavals of the sixteenth and early seventeenth centuries, Old English power and influence held sway. In the post-Reformation takeover of parochial glebe-lands, Protestant immigrants were introduced into the county, often by the existing landowners. In the middle of the seventeenth century there were at least 1,200 clearly defined settlement communities. However, the aftermath of the Cromwellian wars had a significant effect on settlement and land-ownership. The new conquerors were efficient and bureaucratic, introducing comprehensive identification and demarcation of existing property holdings through the Civil and Down Surveys, before going on to reward their soldiers and adventurers with grants of lands. While Clonmel strengthened its position as the centre of administration, new settlers became a significant element in such towns as Golden and Clogheen, as opposed to Fethard and Tipperary Town or the more established towns of the Butler hegemony, such as Carrick-on-Suir and Thurles. Throughout the county, the old landowners were obliged to make themselves known to the Revenue at Limerick or Clonmel before they and their families were forcibly removed to Connacht and their lands confiscated. Most of the major landowners complied, with the exception of the Earl of Ormond, his allies and closest kinsmen. The Restoration of 1660 saw the return of the Earl, now with the title of Duke of Ormond, and the construction in 1675 of a new courthouse for the Palatinate in the centre of Clonmel. This was perhaps a gesture of determination in the face of the new settlers and of reassurance to the interests disrupted by the Cromwellian takeover. The building itself, now known as the Main Guard, is of special interest in that it expresses new ideas of urban design and classicism in architectural design and, while introducing new technology, also incorporates elements reminiscent of medieval construction ***(fig. 10)***. Its recent restoration has revealed that its construction involved the reuse of stone taken from the Cistercian abbey at Inishlounaght, a few miles upstream, which had been suppressed in the Reformation.

(fig. 10)
MAIN GUARD
Sarsfield Street/
Mitchell Street,
Clonmel
(1675)

The court and administration of the Tipperary Palatinate was housed in the Main Guard, one of the finest examples of seventeenth-century public architecture in Ireland. It incorporates dressed stone work probably taken from the Cistercian abbey of Inishlounaght, a few miles to the west.

(fig. 11)
MELDRUM HOUSE
Meldrum
(1622, extended c. 1730)

Meldrum House is a good example of a multi-period country house. The early seventeenth-century right-hand block has a dated coat of arms over its doorway, while the later block has the typical features of an eighteenth-century house.

Some of the great landowning families were later restored to their lands, but most were not, and the effect was to remove traditional patronage of the arts from the older settlements and their inhabitants. The late seventeenth century saw an uneasy equilibrium established in which some displaced landowners re-established themselves on lands adjacent to their earlier holdings ***(fig. 11)***. The result was a complex pattern of new settlers, old landholders who had retained their lands, some who had their lands restored and re-located earlier landholders, some of who had returned from Connacht. Crucial to the development of South Tipperary in the eighteenth and nineteenth centuries was the survival of minor branches of the Butler family who had remained Catholic, under the protection of the Ormond Palatinate, and were mainly concentrated around Cahir, Fethard and Kilcash, near Carrick-on-Suir.

The Cromwellian settlement brought new perspectives on ownership and with it the desire to create integrated demesne landscapes. Many of the old evolved patterns were replaced by, or incorporated into, new designed landscapes enclosed behind high walls. Their perspective demanded that land be productive, resulting in the exploitation of the mature woodlands and the intensification of mining activity. Elements of the older landscape, from roads and bridges, to lanes, hedges and ditches, still survive today to delineate old parish and manorial boundaries ***(figs. 12-13)***.

(fig. 12)
OLD BRIDGE
Carrick-on-Suir
(c. 1450)

One of Ireland's most intact medieval structures, Old Bridge was built in the mid-fifteenth century, connecting the medieval walled town with its suburb, Carrickbeg, across the River Suir. The piers have pedestrian refuges.

(fig. 13)
SIR THOMAS'S BRIDGE
Ferryhouse/
Twomilebridge
(1690)

This bridge, one of the oldest spanning the River Suir, to the east of Clonmel, was erected by Sir Thomas Osborne to connect his estates on either side of the river. The fortified house of Tickincor stands beside the bridge on the County Waterford bank.

The Eighteenth Century

The eighteenth century is often characterised as the Age of Improvement. Emerging industrialisation and the impact of the Enlightenment are usually seen as the twin engines of change in this period of European history. In South Tipperary, as in much of Ireland, these dynamics were filtered through a society that had undergone a highly complex reconstruction. In practical terms, in the early eighteenth century, Ireland was criss-crossed by a network of turnpike roads, opening up formerly isolated areas and linking them to centres of governance and trade. The Maps of the Roads of Ireland (1778) by Taylor and Skinner, show that the land-ownership pattern had stabilised, identifying no fewer than 184 landed properties in South Tipperary. The estates, large and small, featured versions of the 'Big House' and its attendant lands. These holdings would have reflected the uneasy stability that had emerged at the end of the seventeenth century, an accommodation that had both religious and ethnic dimensions. The anti-Catholic Penal Laws were in force and the century held an undercurrent of religious antagonism that was to emerge in full blood in the following century. Yet the Catholic interest survived both in town and country, with a strong mercantile strand in the urban centres, and a persistent presence on the land. One can see in this the real, though diminishing, influence of the Butler hegemony. In many ways, the architecture of Tipperary in the eighteenth century reflects the social and economic structure, as it represents all strands of the population of the time.

The term 'Big House' covers a wide range and scale of buildings, just as the estates these houses occupied varied greatly in size. In South Tipperary, most would fit Maurice Craig's definition as the property of significant and usually resident landlords, rather than referring to the size of the houses. Their character reflects their origins: many of the earliest houses, such as Ardfinnan or Killenure, were built beside, or incorporated, an older fortified structure, while others, such as Marlfield and Knocklofty ***(figs. 14-20)***, were statements of new proprietorship. It is almost impossible to classify some of the more complex adaptations of earlier buildings. Ardfinnan Castle features a medieval cylindrical keep, with a Georgian wing added to

(fig. 14)
MARLFIELD HOUSE
Marlfield
(c.1790)

This Palladian-style country house was built by Col. John Bagwell, M.P. It was rebuilt with a flat roof in 1925 after the centre block was burned in the Troubles two years earlier. The Bagwell family owned much of Clonmel town in the nineteenth century and returned members to Parliament.

(fig. 15)
MARLFIELD HOUSE

Richard Turner designed this curvilinear glasshouse in the mid-nineteenth century. One of the largest attached to a private house, its low curved roof is supported internally by imitation palm trees in cast-iron.

(fig. 16)
MARLFIELD HOUSE

The fine neo-classical entrance gates, incorporating gate lodges, to Marlfield House were designed by William Tinsley in 1833. The gates, the finest nineteenth-century example in the county, are sited in Marlfield village, which is very much a demesne creation.

(fig. 17)
KNOCKLOFTY HOUSE
Knocklofty Demesne
(c. 1790, with mainly 19th century additions)

This rambling U-plan country house appears to have a seventeenth-century core, although the main block has features of c. 1790, the wings being slightly later and the single-storey gallery added to the inner side of the forecourt early in the nineteenth century. Curving bays were added to the garden elevation c. 1910. The main entrance is set within an elaborate porch.
It was the home of the Hely-Hutchinsons, Earls of Donoughmore, one of whom ran for Parliament in the nineteenth century on a Catholic Emancipation ticket.

(fig. 18)
KNOCKLOFTY HOUSE

The library displays some fine plasterwork detailing. The gallery is similar to that in Kilcooly Abbey.

KNOCKLOFTY HOUSE

(fig. 19)
KNOCKLOFTY HOUSE
Knocklofty Demesne
(c. 1780)

The west gate at Knocklofty has high quality stone details evident in the crowned lions' heads to the frieze of the piers.

(fig. 20)
KNOCKLOFTY HOUSE
Knocklofty Demesne
(c. 1820)

This somewhat later gate lodge stands inside the fine late eighteenth-century gates at Knocklofty. It has an unusual split-level form.

a rectangular late medieval tower house, and another tower added in the nineteenth century ***(fig. 21)***. Kiltinan Castle is a three-storey house built in the eighteenth and nineteenth centuries between two medieval towers ***(figs. 22-24)***. Barne Park, dating to c. 1730, was given a dormer storey c. 1870. It has an elaborate entrance doorway, similar to Furness, Co. Kildare, the latter ascribed to the architect Francis Bindon ***(fig. 25)***. Thomastown Castle and Kilcooly Abbey, two of the largest houses, were built close to medieval Augustinian and Cistercian monasteries. The house at Thomastown, now in ruins, was begun in 1670 as a two-storey brick building designed to enhance the relationship of house and garden. It overlooked an enclosed garden of statues and walks, with oculi cut into the brick wall to allow special views to the wider landscape. The house was added to in the early eighteenth century and enlarged and transformed into a castellated mansion in the nineteenth century ***(see figs. 84-5)***.

(fig. 21)
ARDFINNAN CASTLE
Ardfinnan
(c. 1200, with later additions)

This is one of the county's earliest castles, from the reign of King John (1166-1216), showing evidence of many phases of construction between the late twelfth century and the late nineteenth century. It has a fifteenth-century tower house, with later blocks added, all within the remains of the original castle enclosure. It was built to guard an important crossing point on the River Suir.

(fig. 23)
KILTINAN CASTLE

Front elevation.

(fig. 22)
KILTINAN CASTLE
Kiltinan
(c. 1215, with later additions)

Dramatically sited on a bluff overlooking the Clashawley River, Kiltinan Castle was probably begun by Philip of Worcester c.1215, when he was granted the lands. It has many similarities with Ardfinnan Castle, although Kiltinan has larger elevations.

(fig. 25)
BARNE PARK
Barn Demesne
(c. 1730, altered c. 1870)

The French chateau-style roof of the house is an addition of the late nineteenth century. The ornate doorway is similar to that at Furness, Co. Kildare, on a house attributed to the architect Francis Bindon. Barne Park possibly incorporates a seventeenth-century house.

(fig. 24)
KILTINAN CASTLE
Kiltinan
(1842)

The southern gate to Kiltinan, facing the road to Kilsheelan, was an RIC barracks for part of its life. Its design and detailing reflect the nature of the country house that it serves.

The new social and economic order is most visible in the grand architecture of the period. The Cashel Palace, built for Archbishop Theophilus Bolton in 1732 and designed by Sir Edward Lovett Pearce, is a fine Palladian house, built of rose-coloured brick, on a site at the foot of the Rock of Cashel ***(figs. 26-7)***. Bolton added a library, which bears his name, to one side, a precursor to the later structure in the grounds of the Cathedral. Dundrum is another architecturally important house built mainly in the early part of the century ***(fig. 28)***. It was originally a storey lower, the top floor being a well-executed addition. The principal façade, with high quality stonework, is seven bays wide with a central breakfront and a fine door case. A two-storey stable-yard, built a century later, was constructed stylistically to harmonise with the house in a way that expresses the integration of the practical and the aesthetic, the ideal of demesne development in the eighteenth century.

(fig. 26)
CASHEL PALACE HOTEL
Main Street,
Cashel
(1732)

The former palace of the Church of Ireland archbishops of Cashel is one of the key works of Sir Edward Lovett Pearce. It has two elegant façades with high quality details, brick to the street and limestone to the garden. The interior has an elegant carved timber staircase. Shouldered door surrounds and panelled wainscoting are also a feature in this house.

CASHEL PALACE HOTEL

The staircase newels are fluted Corinthian columns.

CASHEL PALACE HOTEL

There is fine stone detailing in the window surrounds, string course and cornice.

(fig. 27)
CASHEL PALACE HOTEL
Main Street,
Cashel
(c. 1750)

A pretty gate lodge adorns the approach to the Cashel Palace, its low size and Gothic door and window openings being in stark contrast to surrounding buildings.

DUNDRUM HOUSE

(fig. 28)
DUNDRUM HOUSE
Dundrum
(c. 1730,
altered c. 1890)

An elegant perron staircase gives access to the piano nobile of this Palladian house, perhaps designed by Sir Edward Lovett Pearce for the Maude family. The top floor was added c. 1890, changing its proportions, particularly in relation to the wings. The building was built in red brick and rendered in the early twentieth century.

(fig. 29)
CLONBROGAN HOUSE
Clonbrogan
(c. 1700)

This is a rare example of a small early eighteenth-century farmhouse. There are attic windows high in the gables and, unusually, only one original rear window.

MANGANSTOWN HOUSE
Mauganstown
(1648, refenestrated c. 1750)

In contrast with Clonbrogan, Manganstown was occupied by Catholic farmers, who fought in the 1798 rebellion. Its appearance, a debased version of Palladian, apparently masks a seventeenth-century house with a slightly-battered rear wall and a plaque to the facade, dated 1643, commemorating Richard Butler and his wife E. L.

MANGANSTOWN HOUSE

The armorial plaque on the façade.

(fig. 30)
CORRABELLA HOUSE
Corrabella
(c. 1780)

Corrabella, near Newcastle, is a superb example of a house with slate-hung walls. The porch was formerly gabled.

But the new ideas had far wider influence. The county possesses a wealth of dignified and well-proportioned country residences from this period, the houses of the 'strong farmer', with a particular density of large holdings in the southern baronies of the county. The seventeenth-century plantation might have resulted in a change in land-ownership, but not necessarily in those farming it. Many of the houses of the period were built in a tradition that absorbed ideas of symmetry and the rational ordering of elements within a familiar building technology. Clonbrogan, near Fethard, is a very fine early example ***(fig. 29)***. Built by the Watson family in about 1700, it is a five-bay, two-storey house with an attic storey lit from the gables. The house has a pronounced batter to the rear elevation and has chimneystacks over each gable. Corrabella House, built in the mid-to-late eighteenth century, is typical of many – a plain five-bay, three-storey house with its farmyard to the rear. It is well proportioned, with a good rhythm of windows ***(fig. 30)***. The original door case has been concealed by a later porch. (This is interesting because few early eighteenth-century houses had porches or porticos.) It faces south-west to the Knockmealdowns and has unusually extensive slate-hanging on its front façade and to both sides, with a rendered finish facing the farmyard at the rear. The later porch has also been weather-slated, with some decorative patterns around the parapet.

Slate-hanging, also known as slate-cladding or weather-slating is a feature of the southern counties of Ireland and particularly South Tipperary and appears in some form on many of the more formal rural and urban houses and on some other buildings, such as mills. Apparently originating in the eighteenth century, it is usually applied to only the most

(fig. 31)
1-2 NEW QUAY
Clonmel
(c. 1765)

This pair of houses, on the quayside in Clonmel, has a distinctive slate-hung facade. The first was built by John Christian, a wealthy merchant, and has decorative motifs, one with the lettering 'John Christian Fecit'.

1 NEW QUAY

Decorative details.

exposed walls, facing south-west or facing a body of water. The finish offers a technologically perfect waterproof but breathable cladding. Aesthetically, it is a beautiful finish, textured and with varying planes which reflect the light in different ways and with all the richness and variety of the slate colour, in rain or sunshine. The house built by John Christian in Clonmel, one of a pair of merchants' houses on the quayside and facing south, is unusual in that the slates are cut in decorative panels, one bearing the lettering 'John Christian Fecit', some letters and a date of '176_' now lost ***(fig. 31)***. Another fine urban example is to be seen on Friar Street in Carrick-on-Suir ***(fig. 32)***. The bowed garden elevation of Salisbury, a house near Clonmel, overlooking Marlfield

(fig. 32)
FRIAR STREET
Carrick-on-Suir
(c. 1760)

Like the quayside pair in Clonmel, this house has slate-hung upper floors. One former window has been blocked up and slated over.

Lake, is slate-hung to its southern half and Killough Castle and Templenoe House have slate-hung rear and side elevations ***(fig. 33)***. In Shanrahan graveyard, near Clogheen, there is evidence of weather-slating in an unusual application, on a ruined eighteenth-century church tower: only a few slates survive, but the imprint of others is clearly visible. The exposed south wall of Clonmel's West Gate is another non-domestic instance. Slates used in this technique are small and light, probably often off-cuts or rejects. Traditionally, they are bedded in lime mortar instead of being nailed to laths as in roofing applications, although sometimes this is done to effect patch repairs. The south gable of 22 Gladstone Street, Clonmel, has been recently repaired using the traditional technique.

(fig. 33)
THE GLEBE
Templenoe
(1776-84)

A rectory until 1885, this house near Tipperary Town was formerly called Templenoe House and displays fine slate-hanging to its rear elevation and the rear half of each gable.

In general, the farmyards associated with country houses consist of ranges of agricultural buildings and stable-blocks constructed around two or three sides of a regularly shaped yard ***(fig. 34)***. In most of the more modest examples, the dwelling house forms one side of the yard, and is entered from it. In more prosperous holdings, the house may be turned around so that the visitor approaches a formal entrance away from the workings of the farm, sometimes through an attractive garden area. An orchard could usually be found in the immediate vicinity of the house and yard, along with one or more sheltered paddocks or 'haggards.' The haggard was an integral part of the farming operation and was where newly saved hay was built into ricks or where weaker animals could be allowed out to graze while protected from predators and within easy reach of the farmhouse.

(fig. 34)
BALLYOWEN HOUSE
Newpark
(c. 1760)

Ballyowen House is notable for having good quality outbuildings, one having a dressed limestone bellcote over one gable and another with a classically-inspired pedimented breakfront.

BALLYOWEN HOUSE

(fig. 35)
BALLYOWEN HOUSE
Newpark
(c. 1760)

The Pennef(e)ather family built Ballyowen, near Cashel, a house distinctive for the Venetian arrangement of openings to the ground floor, a feature reminiscent of the Cashel Palace.

(fig. 36)
LONGFIELD HOUSE
Longfield
(c. 1770)

This house is unusual for having bows to all four sides, round to front and back and half-hexagonal to the sides. The doorcase has a heavy block-and-start surround. Charles Bianconi, pioneer of coach travel in Ireland, lived here from 1846 until his death in 1875.

The period of greatest demesne development spanned the transition from the eighteenth to the nineteenth centuries. This period produced a wealth of fine country houses. Ballyowen, built in the 1770s by the Pennefather family, is a five-bay, three-storey house, and has a window arrangement reminiscent of the archbishop's palace in Cashel ***(fig. 35)***. Longfield is an important house of the time with five bays, three storeys and a heavy round-headed doorcase. It is almost baroque in style, having a projecting bow on all four sides ***(fig. 36)***. Anne's Gift, near Fethard, is another fine five-bay, three-storey house, built probably about 1780,

(fig. 37)
MILLGROVE HOUSE
Tincurry
(c. 1770)

The symmetry of the façade is emphasised by the spacing of the openings and especially by the tripartite detailing of the middle bay. The fine flight of steps leads to an elegant Gibbsian doorcase. The house, near Ballylooby, has a bow to the rear, and attic windows to the gables.

(fig. 38)
BALLINGARRANE HOUSE
Ballingarrane
(1797)

This house displays the conceit, common in Ireland, of having the lowest level appear as a half-basement to the front and as the ground floor to the rear. The building has a stairs return at the rear.

with a rendered exterior and a hipped roof. Millgrove House has two storeys over a half-basement, a fine cut-stone doorcase, and an elliptical bow to the rear ***(fig. 37)***. Ballingarrane House (1797), formerly known as Summerville, is said to be possibly an early work by the well-known architect, Richard Morrison. It is also a five-bay, two-storey house, with later two-storey wings ***(fig. 38)***. Its dower house, Glenconnor House, was built at the same time and has a small, later, Ionic portico to an otherwise quite plain building ***(fig. 39)***.

Developments were not confined to the building of houses. New demesne landscapes were created, using new technologies to maintain water features and to plant semi-mature trees to create an immediate effect. Estate bridges, boathouses and follies were features of these demesnes ***(fig. 40)***.

(fig. 39)
GLENCONNOR HOUSE
Glenconnor
(1797)

Glenconnor was erected as a dower house for Ballingarrane. The wings were added c. 1885 and the portico in 1904. It has an elaborately decorated hall.

(fig. 40)
THE GUGGY
Knocklofty Demesne
(c. 1820)

Follies are a feature of many demesnes, this example being octagonal in plan with a domed brick roof, and sited on a hill overlooking Knocklofty House.

The impetus for improvement also had a profound influence on urban life. The network of roads, the construction of bridges and the improvement of waterways meant that the produce of the rich farmlands could be freely traded ***(fig. 41)***. These benefits fell unevenly on the towns of South Tipperary. Fethard, an important walled settlement in medieval times, accommodated Cromwell in his campaigns in the county, and later quartered Williamite troops, but by the eighteenth century had become a relative backwater, probably due to the growing prominence of Clonmel. Nonetheless, it retains interesting buildings of the period, such as Fethard Rectory, just north

(fig. 41)
NEWCASTLE BRIDGE
Moloughnewtown/ Clashganny West
(c. 1770)

This fine five-arch bridge spans the River Suir, with the Knockmealdown Mountains as a scenic backdrop.

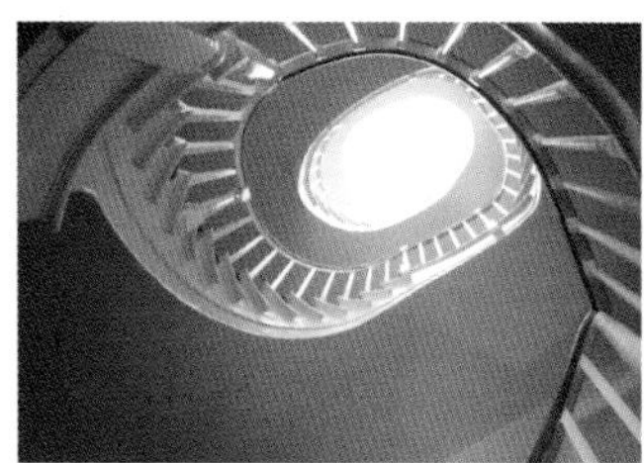

FETHARD RECTORY

(fig. 42)
FETHARD RECTORY
Fethard
(1796)

The wider spaces to each side of the middle bay, coupled with a low door case, give this former rectory an unusual appearance. The house, which may have a seventeenth-century core, has an attic lit by windows high in the gables and by the diminutive dormer over the front façade. There is a Rococo-style staircase in the entrance hall.

(fig. 43)
MAIN STREET
Fethard
(c. 1800)

One of the finest townhouses in South Tipperary, this former presbytery displays fine render detailing, especially in the pediments and cornices to its windows and porch.

(fig. 44)
BURKE STREET
Fethard
(c. 1790)

Superb engaged Corinthian columns are the main glory of this shopfront, which has been described as one of the best classical shopfronts in Ireland.

(fig. 45)
ABYMILL THEATRE
Abbeyville,
Fethard
(1791)

Part of this former flour mill was converted to a theatre in 1988. It was built on the site of the south range of the adjacent medieval Augustinian abbey.

of the town, the former parochial house on Main Street and O'Shea's shop on Burke Street ***(figs. 42-4)***. The almshouses/tholsel building on Main Street, mentioned earlier, lost its philanthropic function c.1750, when the ground floor of the building became a market-house. This appears to have involved the construction of an arcade, as well as the blocking of most of the original windows. The Abbey Mill, built on part of the domestic buildings of the fourteenth-century Augustinian friary, was built in 1791 ***(fig. 45)***. Cashel, a much larger town, took time to recover commercially from its sacking by Lord Inchiquin in 1647, although its fine cathedral (1763), possibly incorporating the fabric of the medieval parish church of St John, and the archbishop's palace (1731), are fine examples of eighteenth-century architecture. The front façade of the cathedral is a well-executed neo-classical composition by John Roberts. Richard Morrison added the tower in 1812 ***(figs. 46-7)***. Carrick-on-Suir remained prosperous, sustained by its position on the River Suir, the main trading route between Waterford and Clonmel, and developed into a self-sufficient trading town. Cahir offered no resistance to Cromwell and remained part of the Butler estates into the nineteenth century. The town was redesigned and the Square given its present form in the late 1770s and early 1780s. Tipperary Town suffered during the wars of the seventeenth century when its grammar school was burnt, although it was rebuilt in 1702. Some improvements were carried through in the eighteenth century, notably the building of stone houses to replace cabins, for example on St Michael's Street and O'Brien Street, and the construction of shops and commercial premises on Main Street and Limerick Street. A new Roman Catholic Mass house or unofficial chapel was also constructed in the town about this time, but the primary landlords, the Smith-Barry family, seem to have shown little interest in the town until the second half of the nineteenth century.

The principal beneficiary of the eighteenth-century period of relative stability was the town of Clonmel. A walled medieval town, it was the only town in Ireland successfully to resist Cromwell's assault, the Lord Protector losing about 2,000 troops there, the heaviest defeat in his military career, and being forced to agree terms with the townspeople.

There were Quaker communities in South Tipperary from the end of the seventeenth century, a meetinghouse, now demolished, having been constructed at Peter Street in 1699 and a burial ground at nearby O'Neill Street established in 1709. Members of this community were instrumental in establishing a thriving woollen industry at Carrick-on-Suir, which provided the capital for their substantial milling enterprises in Clonmel, and later Cahir, Carrick-on-Suir, Clogheen and other places ***(fig. 48)***. Many of the large eighteenth and nineteenth-century houses in these towns were built for Quaker merchants, and their construction employed some of the most notable architects of their eras. Clonmel was also prominent in the butter and bacon trades, in addition to brewing and distilling. Its river frontage was lined with prosperous merchants' houses and large warehouses and mills. The John Christian house, mentioned above, is a fine example of the merchant housing along the quay. Other important merchants included Stephen Moore, who is reported to have exported 7,000 tons of flour to Dublin in 1771, and Robert Joseph Grubb, who was to become a leading merchant in the following decades. He set up a milling business in the town in 1772, and in 1778 his great mills on Suir Island were constructed. The Grubb family is still involved in the county's commerce today, albeit on a smaller scale.

Several of the buildings on O'Connell Street are of eighteenth-century date, but some contain sixteenth and early seventeenth-century fabric. Wolfe Tone Street, leading towards the graveyard of Old St Mary's Church, features fine tall houses built in the late eighteenth Century. The town was subject to the most intense speculative development pressure characterised by

(fig. 46)
CATHEDRAL OF SAINT JOHN THE BAPTIST AND ST PATRICK'S ROCK
John Street,
Cashel
(1763-88)

The Georgian cathedral in Cashel, on the site of the medieval parish church of St John, took twenty-five years to build. Its west gable front is a very distinguished neo-classical composition, the centrepiece of which is a meticulously detailed aedicule. Curiously, the building's long sides are differently detailed, the north having pilasters with Ionic capitals and the south having rusticated pilasters more in the manner of quoins. The tower and spire were added by Richard Morrison in the 1780s.

(fig. 47)
CATHEDRAL OF SAINT JOHN THE BAPTIST AND ST PATRICK'S ROCK

The interior of the cathedral was remodelled in 1866 by William Atkins.

(fig. 48)
CASTLEGRACE MILL
Castlegrace
(c. 1790)

The enormous mill building at Castlegrace has five storeys and twenty-five bays. It is part of a complex that includes a nineteenth-century country house and smaller millers' houses.

abnormally high ground rents. One of the factors here seems to have been the disposal of the Ormond properties within the town in the early years of the century. The courthouse of the Palatinate continued in use until the Palatinate was abolished. The building was converted into a tholsel and then into a barracks whence it derives the name Main Guard by which it is known. In 1766, the notorious trial and execution of Father Nicholas Sheehy, based on trumped up charges of murder and sedition, took place at the site. This event encapsulated the atmosphere of sectarian tension of the time, with prominent members of the new order instrumental in the judicial killing.

The restructuring of society in the seventeenth century also produced a demand for symbols of the new order, in the form of civil and religious buildings. The gaol was constructed in 1787 to the design of William Robinson and its gateway and most of the precinct walls survive today, although the main buildings were demolished in the late twentieth century.

In the particular circumstances of eighteenth-century Ireland, the drive to create a more enlightened society had a strongly sectarian character. While the Restoration and its limited restitution had mitigated the impact of the seventeenth-century upheavals, anti-Catholic enthusiasms were diluted rather than removed. The power of education to improve the condition of the 'lower orders' of the population and to lead towards a more productive and orderly society, was an ideal espoused by Enlightenment thinkers throughout Europe. In the colonial context of the time in Ireland, the idea appealed to the more socially and politically aware among the ruling élite, and provided a focus for public benefaction. There was also a strong drive among the newest settlers to remove the Catholic 'threat' for all time. These twin motives lay behind a series of educational initiatives, commencing in the latter years of the seventeenth century. Erasmus Smith, who had been granted extensive lands in west Tipperary, decided to use some of his property to endow three grammar schools for the education of the sons of his Protestant tenants. The Abbey Grammar School in Tipperary Town was established next to the site of the medieval Augustinian friary and opened in 1680, being destroyed and rebuilt shortly after. It continues in use as a school, though it serves Catholics as well as Protestants and is now known as the Abbey School ***(see fig. 131)***.

Among the initiatives pioneered in the eighteenth century was that of the Charter Schools. These were built under the aegis of the Incorporated Society in Dublin for Promoting English Protestant Schools in Ireland. They were to provide for children of poor Catholic parents, 'those whose economic misfortune placed them at the disposal of the pious', to house them, train them in useful trades and to raise them to live virtuous lives. The charter school in Clonmel, founded in 1748, and now known as Silverspring House, was to the forefront of this activity. Architecturally one of the best surviving examples, it was built under the patronage of Sir Charles Moore and John Dawson. It became a day school in 1821 and is now privately owned. The pedigree of the building is unclear, being described by Maurice Craig as a most important early eighteenth-century house but at the same time having a plan characteristic of a seventeenth-century house ***(fig. 49)***. A charter school was also built in Cashel in 1751, under the patronage of the Archbishop of Cashel, the Corporation of Cashel and W. Palliser. It was closed in 1829, demolished in the mid-twentieth century and now only the master's house survives ***(fig. 50)***.

The Protestant Church had maintained the diocesan organisation, and, as in medieval times, its income was derived from the land attached to the Sees. Revenues rose steadily through the eighteenth century. But a combination of lay indifference and clerical neglect took their toll, and the Church suffered a dramatic decline in the latter years of the century. In 1711 the Board of First Fruits was established, composed chiefly of members of the hierarchy, to buy up impropriations (where church tithes had been assigned to laymen), purchase glebes (land set aside for the maintenance of the clergy) and glebe houses, and to build and repair parish churches. During the 1777-8 session of the Irish parliament, a system of annual grants to the Board of First Fruits was instigated to encourage the construction of churches and glebe-houses. By 1780, the Board had purchased glebes for sixteen benefices, assisted the building of forty-five glebe-houses, and bought impropriate tithes for fourteen incumbents ***(fig. 51)***. Nationally, by 1829, almost 700 churches were built, rebuilt or enlarged by the Board. South Tipperary featured in these developments. The large churches at Clonmel and Fethard are medieval buildings of

(fig. 49)
SILVERSPRING HOUSE
St Patrick's Road, Clonmel
(1747-8)

The Incorporated Society in Dublin for Promoting English Protestant Schools in Ireland established the charter school at Clonmel. This is one of the best preserved examples and may it has been suggested that its archaic, late seventeenth-century-style appearance may indicate that it was built to a design of fifty years earlier for a house or a barracks. These schools had classrooms, dormitories, an infirmary and a master's room. It closed as a school in 1823 and was home to Charles Bianconi until 1846, who gave it its name.

(fig. 50)
CASHEL CHARTER SCHOOL
Charter-school land, Cashel
(1751)

The Archbishop of Cashel, the Corporation of Cashel, and Mr W. Palliser were the patrons of the charter school at Cashel. It was closed in 1829. The building, attributed to Richard Castle, was demolished in the mid-twentieth century.

(fig. 51)
GLEBE HOUSE
Kilvemnon
(1781-93)

The present front façade of this impressive former rectory is a storey higher than the rear and it seems that the building has been reoriented. It is pleasantly set back from the road, near Mullinahone.

the thirteenth century and were modified in succeeding centuries Each retains its distinctive tower, visible from all approaches ***(figs. 52-6)***. The church at Bansha, erected on the site of a medieval parish church, was extensively renovated in 1793-4 and given its spire in 1814 ***(fig. 57)***. Smaller rural churches were built at Lismalin and Ballybeg (Tullaghmelan) ***(fig. 58)***.

(fig. 52)
ST MARY'S CHURCH OF IRELAND
Mary Street, Clonmel
(c. 1400, with 19th century additions and alterations)

Old St Mary's, as it is known, has a distinctive octagonal tower and clearly visible evidence of a complex architectural history. It is an early thirteenth-century foundation. The upper part of the tower dates to c. 1805 and other works include Joseph Welland's rebuilding of the nave in 1857 and his son's addition of a transept in 1864. Clonmel's medieval town wall forms the north and west boundaries of the surrounding graveyard.

(fig. 53)
ST MARY'S CHURCH OF IRELAND

View from the south-west.

(fig. 54)
ST MARY'S CHURCH OF IRELAND

The Interior.

(fig. 55)
HOLY TRINITY CHURCH OF IRELAND
Main Street,
Fethard
(13th century, altered 1785 and 1815)

The immense tower of the medieval parish church of Fethard is the town's dominant landmark. The present church occupies the nave of the original, the chancel and Lady Chapel being ruined and roofless.

(fig. 56)
HOLY TRINITY CHURCH OF IRELAND

The interior of Holy Trinity is remarkably austere, the armorial plaques of the town's leading families, and a few memorials and grave-slabs adding a decorative element.

(fig. 57)
ST MARY'S CHURCH OF IRELAND
Bansha
(1718 and 1793-4)

The fine octagonal tower and spire at Bansha were added in 1793-4 and the castellated gables are reminiscent of the later St Paul's Church in Cahir. The church stands on the site of, and may incorporate fabric from, the medieval parish church of Bansha.

(fig. 58)
TULLAGHMELAN CHURCH OF IRELAND
Ballybeg (Tullaghmelan)
(c. 1780)

This average-size rural church, near Ardfinnan, has features typical of such Board of First Fruits churches. The simple rectangular nave, small chancel and west tower were supplemented in the 1860s by the addition of the dressed limestone vestry. The Massey family paid for the interior, executed c. 1870, which is based on Salisbury Cathedral.

LISMALIN CHURCH OF IRELAND
Lismalin
(c. 1450, refurbished 1715-16 and 1796)

The evocative ruins of Lismalin Church of Ireland incorporate fabric from its medieval precursor.

(fig. 59)
MOANVURRIN
(c. 1800)

Four bays and a hipped roof are typical features of most of the county's lowland vernacular houses. The alignment of chimneystack and entrance indicates a lobby-entry plan, wherein a small wall with a 'spy window' at right angles to the hearth wall forms a lobby to protect the hearth fire from draughts from outside, while allowing the door to be kept open for light and air. This house stands near Drangan.

(fig. 60)
BALLYLYNCH
(c. 1800)

Two-storey thatched houses are very rare in Ireland. This house at Three Bridges, at the edge of Carrick-on-Suir, displays the small square first floor windows often seen in such dwellings. The rounded windbreak with slated roof is an attractive feature of many vernacular houses.

The geological structure of South Tipperary has contributed good building stone, mainly sandstone and limestone, to its inhabitants. In the Clonmel area, for instance, most of the buildings and boundary walls are of sandstone, with limestone being used for finer details or for prominent public buildings. The West Gate and the gaol exemplify this phenomenon ***(see fig. 99)***.

Vernacular dwellings were mainly constructed of these materials, usually with an application of lime rendering. Clay ('mud') was also used, a row of small houses demolished recently in Tipperary Town exhibiting several different techniques of mud walling. This underlines the significance of vernacular architecture to the understanding of Ireland's built heritage. The improvers of the eighteenth century saw the replacement of urban clay-built cabins by stone houses as a mark of progress. Brick only makes an occasional appearance from the eighteenth century onwards, although it became widely used in the nineteenth and twentieth centuries in details such as chimneystacks and some door and window surrounds. Most of the vernacular houses in South Tipperary have a 'lobby-entry' plan form. These houses are notable for having their kitchen hearth chimneystack in line with the front door. Inside the doorway there is a short 'jamb' wall screening the hearth fire from the doorway and often pierced by a small 'spy' window, which enables a person seated at the hearth to see visitors arriving at the door ***(fig. 59)***. Vernacular houses and other buildings are the result of 'designs' handed on through generations, rather than being conceived on a drawing board. In this way their origins are radically different to those of formally designed buildings. The retention of traditional construction techniques, such as local thatching types, is fundamental to the survival of their historic fabric. South Tipperary has almost 100 surviving thatched buildings, most of them three or four-roomed houses, although there are examples of two-storey houses ***(fig. 60)***. The 'Bothán Scóir' in Cashel, which is claimed to be seventeenth century in date, is a diminutive one-roomed house with a hipped, thatched roof, very small window openings and a most interesting traditional interior ***(figs. 61-2)***.

(fig. 61)
BOTHÁN SCÓIR
Clonmel Road,
Cashel
(c. 1750)

This diminutive vernacular house originally formed part of a row of similar buildings at the edge of the town of Cashel. It is remarkably well preserved and is now a museum of traditional life.

(fig. 62)
BOTHÁN SCÓIR

The highly interesting interior retains its original roughly-hewn roof timbering, without a ceiling, so that the thatch is everywhere visible above the ribs or small timbers that run across the backs of the couples or roof trusses. The hearth is to the right, with the traditional metal crane.

The Nineteenth Century

The nineteenth century in South Tipperary was a period of transformation and revolution. It brought changes in transport infrastructure, economic boom and decline, the emergence of Catholic and nationalist interests, and a revolution in landholding. All left indelible traces on the physical and social landscapes ***(figs. 63-5)***.

The ending of the Napoleonic wars created major difficulties for agriculture and industry in South Tipperary but also provided an entrepreneurial opportunity. The county had been a major supplier of horses to the British army. Charles (Carlo) Bianconi (1786-1875) had originally been apprenticed by his father to an itinerant art dealer and was brought to Dublin in 1802. Later, he moved to Clonmel where, with backing from his father, he established his own business, operating as a gilder. He then established a coaching service operating from the town, initially helped by the sharp drop in demand and price that enabled him to purchase horses cheaply. The service carried people, goods and mail and transformed the country's transport, trade and communications. His first coaching venture, in July 1815, was a passenger service between Clonmel and Cahir, later expanded to Cork, Wexford, Waterford and thereafter throughout the country. He established his headquarters in Clonmel at what became Hearn's Hotel. Ever the entrepreneur, Bianconi became aware of the emerging potential of the railways and, notwithstanding the threat to his coaching service, he invested in the Waterford-Limerick railway.

As in the rest of Ireland, transport in Tipperary was revolutionised by the coming of the railways. A study carried out by the Irish Railway Commissioners in 1837 recommended that a main line be constructed from Dublin to Cork via Cashel, intersecting with a Waterford-Limerick line passing through Carrick on Suir, Clonmel, Cahir and Tipperary Town. Local

(fig. 63)
ARDFINNAN BRIDGE
Ardfinnan
(c. 1800)

The river scene at Ardfinnan is dominated by the multi-period castle begun in the reign of King John and guarding the crossing of the Suir, a place which has had a bridge since before 1311. The long thirteen-arch bridge shows evidence of widening to its east side and may incorporate medieval and/or seventeenth-century fabric. The double-pile building at the end of the bridge was formerly part of a large wool factory established in 1869 and operated by Mulcahy, Redmond and Co.

(fig. 64)
WILFORD BRIDGE
Shangarry
(1866)

A small three-arch bridge over the King's River displays high quality craftsmanship in its contrasting stonework - rock-faced parapets and arch spandrels, and finely dressed string course, arch voussoirs and round cutwaters.

(fig. 65)
KINGSTON BRIDGE
Barnahown
(1859)

Charles Tarrant and W.H. Deane, the county surveyors of Tipperary and Waterford, are named on this plaque, set into the parapet of a single-arch bridge spanning the Araglin River on the border of the two counties. M. Barr and Michael Byrne were the contractors.

politics ensured that the line passed through Thurles rather than Cashel, to the great disadvantage of the latter. The great period of railway building for the county was between 1844 and 1857. Further branch lines were built in 1879-80 between Clonmel and Thurles, and the connection of Cashel to the main line at Goold's Cross, in 1904, some fifty years after the construction of the main lines. Construction coincided with a period of great upheaval while the horror of the Great Famine was at its peak. The construction of the railway was seen to have several important strategic roles, as well as its intended support for agriculture, trade and industry. It linked important military barracks at Clonmel, Tipperary and Templemore, providing a means of ensuring security throughout the county. Construction was also a useful means of relieving local distress and suppressing discontent by providing work for many displaced labourers, Tipperary being regarded as the 'most disturbed' county in Ireland at that time. For over a century, the railway played a pivotal role in the movement of people and goods to and from the county and most stations had goods yards for handling livestock, bloodstock and sugar beet.

The railway also had an important symbolic value, which was reflected in the quality of the associated engineering and architectural works. Stations and staff housing, bridges and signal cabins, workers' cottages, water-towers and goods sheds were all constructed to high standards. Crisply detailed cut stone, elaborate timber bargeboards and decorative cast-iron elements typified the buildings along the lines. The station at Clonmel ***(figs. 66-7)*** was designed in 1852, probably by J.S. Mulvany, builder of Broadstone Station in Dublin. Other stations at Tipperary, Dundrum, Fethard, Goold's Cross and

(fig. 66)
CLONMEL RAILWAY STATION
Thomas Street, Clonmel
(1852)

The restrained but attractive station building at Clonmel has a tower which is very similar to that at Connolly Station, Dublin. Described as 'robustly Italianate', the building was possibly designed by J.S. Mulvany.

(fig. 67)
CLONMEL RAILWAY STATION

A trackside view of the station, with its iron footbridge of 1886.

CLONMEL RAILWAY STATION

Plaque to pedestrian footbridge.

CLONMEL RAILWAY STATION

Signal cabin.

(fig. 68)
FARRANALEEN RAILWAY STATION
Farranaleen
(1880)

Its single-storey size reflects the status of the station on the branch line between Clonmel and Thurles. Rock-faced limestone quoins, dressed limestone chimneystacks and carved timber bargeboards add decorative detail. The station has a small, well-kept goods shed, its original platforms, and a cast-iron milepost. This railway line was closed in 1964.

FARRANALEEN RAILWAY STATION

(fig. 69)
KENNEDY'S BAR
Clonoulty Churchquarter
(c. 1860)

Goold's Cross, a rural stop on the Dublin to Cork railway line, had a hotel that would be more appropriate for a town. The retention of timber sash windows and the decorative render, particularly to the gabled projection, are attractive features.

(*fig. 70*)
CAHIR RAILWAY STATION
Church Street,
Cahir
(1852)

W.G. Murray chose the Tudor Revival style for the station at Cahir, on the Waterford to Limerick line. The building has well crafted limestone walls and details.

Farranaleen vary greatly in design ***(figs. 68-9)***. The station at Cahir was designed by W.G. Murray in 1851 ***(fig. 70)***. The railway line from Cahir to Limerick crosses the Suir by means of the remarkable viaduct at Cahir. Constructed between 1851 and 1853 of wrought-iron box girders, it is an especially fine example of bridge engineering ***(fig. 71)***. There are also many examples of well-executed cut-stone bridges serving the various lines.

SUIR BRIDGE

(*fig. 71*)
SUIR BRIDGE
Caherabbey Upper/
Townparks (Caher par.),
Cahir
(1852)

William Le Fanu specified steel box girders for this impressive viaduct over the River Suir at Cahir. The central span is 45m (150ft) and the others are 16m (52ft). The castellations echo those of the nearby medieval Cahir Castle. It is one of the most significant engineering achievements in Ireland.

The Slieveardagh coalfield, between Killenaule and The Commons, was first developed in the 1650s, and was exploited sporadically until the mine closed in the 1980s. The coal extracted from the mines was said to be of good quality, but the seams proved difficult and expensive to work. Mining began as landlord ventures, with proprietors such as W.P. Barker in Kilcooly, Charles Langley in Coalbrook and Sir Vere Hunt in Glengoole opening pits on their estates; although as early as 1824, the Mining Company of Ireland leased most of the area from local landowners. Hunt founded a town c. 1813, which he optimistically called New Birmingham, intending it to be an important manufacturing centre. He chose the location on the basis of the adjacent deposits of coal in the Slieveardagh Hills. The investor obtained patents to hold two-weekly markets and twelve fairs per year. He engaged the services of an architect for the village chapel. In 1837, however, Samuel Lewis, in his Topographical Dictionary of Ireland, noted that the village of fifty houses was 'comparatively deserted,' and that the markets and fairs had ceased. The village as it stands today gives little indication of its roots as a proto-industrial town. There had been considerable demand for the coal to fire the grain-drying kilns in the great mills of Clonmel, and for malting throughout the county. The later decline in milling impacted upon demand for Killenaule coal, while the diminishing depth of the seam reduced the viability of extraction. By 1889, some of the largest mines were only partially worked. The remnants of these endeavours are still to be seen, often as abandoned relics in the agricultural landscape. A purpose-built mining town consisting of twenty-five houses was founded in 1828 at Mardyke, known locally as 'The Found', but the pit closed in 1833. Engine houses, which accommodated steam-powered machines to pump water out of the mines, survive at Mardyke and Knockalonga, with venting chimneys here and at several other locations ***(figs. 72-3)***. Other clusters of houses were created to serve other mines, quarries and mills. Kilmore, Ballinderry and Kilbeg all began life as mill clusters. Such clusters were somewhat alien, often developing a strong group identity in contrast with their surrounding rural communities. In 1848 William Smith O'Brien came to The Commons colliery to drum up support for the Young Irelander Rebellion, demanding better pay and conditions for the miners. The constabulary took refuge in the Widow McCormack's farmhouse, since known as 'The War House' and the early arrival of reinforcements put an end to the affair ***(fig. 74)***.

(fig. 72)
MARDYKE
(1824)

Engine houses and chimneys are dotted throughout the Slieveardagh Hills, where coalmining was carried out as early as the seventeenth century. A colliery and a mining village, complete with a school, were established at Mardyke, reputedly the site of the first coal-working of the modern era. The colliery closed in 1919.

(fig. 73)
THE STEEPLE OF COPPER
Ballingarry Lower
(c. 1830)

This square-plan chimney, a major landmark in the coal district, marks the site of a long-gone colliery at the hamlet of Copper, near Ballingarry.

(fig. 74)
THE WAR HOUSE
Farranrory Upper
(c. 1845)

The modest house of Widow McCormick became the site of the main action in the aborted rising of 1848. In response to the assembling of a force of Young Irelanders at Ballingarry, led by William Smith O'Brien, James Stephens and Terence Bellew McManus, a party of police was despatched to the area. Mistakenly assuming up to 5000 opponents, the police fled to this house, where they were besieged and took the widow's children as hostages. In response to stone throwing during the subsequent negotiations, the police shot and killed a man, the siege then being called off. The site is now a National Monument.

(fig. 75)
KILTINAN
(c. 1880)

The promoters of a brick-works at Kiltinan, near Fethard, had invested on the assumption that they would be provided with a siding off the Clonmel-Thurles railway line. They were to be disappointed and abandoned the project, having only built the chimney.

(fig. 76)
BALLYLUSKY
(Magowry par.)
(c. 1820)

This is a rare example of a double limekiln, standing near Drangan. Crushed lime was burned into powder in these structures and used as fertiliser for the land or as mortar for building work.

The county also had other extractive industries, such as copper mines near Hollyford and brickworks at Kiltinan, only the chimney for the latter being constructed ***(fig. 75)***. There were also limekilns dispersed through the county for the production of lime ***(fig. 76)***.

The early years of the century saw a continuation and intensification of the growth in the agricultural and industrial production of the late eighteenth century, fuelled by the demands of the Napoleonic wars. The economic prosperity of landed interests was reflected in the continuing and ambitious development of some country houses and demesnes. Also, those towns that had emerged as commercially prosperous manifested their wealth in the building of new houses, shops and public buildings. Overall, however, the picture is one of contrasts, with underlying structural weaknesses that led to conflict as the century progressed.

The Encumbered Estates Acts of 1848-9 facilitated the disposal of estates made insolvent through high rates and declining rental income during the Great Famine, resulting in the transfer of ownership in many cases. As a whole, Tipperary was not a county noted for great estates, landholdings varying considerably in size and value. It has been suggested that the reason for the proliferation of small and low-value estates in the eighteenth and nineteenth centuries lay in the piecemeal and protracted fragmentation of the Butler estates. However, South Tipperary possessed the majority of the larger holdings, located mainly in the barony of Iffa and Offa West, in the lower reaches of the Suir, and the southern baronies also had the greatest continuity of tenure of farms held by the same families.

Towards the end of the eighteenth century, William Barker of Kilcooly created a new lake, excavating several acres of good agricultural land adjacent to his Palladian house. Perhaps the most ambitious example of estate development is that of the Glengall Butlers at Cahir. The second Earl landscaped and planted a two-mile stretch on both banks of the Suir, to create a romantic 'natural' landscape in accordance with the approach of Humphrey Repton, then in vogue. The effect was enhanced by the addition in 1820 of a particularly notable thatched cottage orné, designed by John Nash and called the Swiss Cottage ***(figs. 77-8)***. Nash was also engaged in the design of Shanbally Castle, near Ballyporeen, for Cornelius O'Callaghan, M.P. The largest of Nash's country houses in Ireland, it sat in a landscaped demesne with views of the Galtee and Knockmealdown mountains to the north and south. The house had an unusual design, with a linear sequence of spaces

(fig. 78)
THE SWISS COTTAGE

One of the most important elements of the interior is a rare Dufour wallpaper in the principal ground floor room, with the exotic Rives du Bosphore, depicting the city of Istanbul. A decorative cast-iron fence encloses the garden and continues the natural theme of the cottage.

(fig. 77)
THE SWISS COTTAGE
Kilcommon More (North)
(1810-14)

John Nash was the architect of the best surviving cottage orné in Ireland or Britain, built for the tenth Baron Caher (later the first Earl of Glengall) and his wife. It stands on a bluff overlooking the River Suir at the south end of the parkland behind their main dwelling, Cahir House. This view, from the south-west, highlights the use of tree trunks and vegetation to create the sense of the house growing out of nature. The deliberate irregularity of detailing, especially in the treatment of window heads, is a feature of the house.

(fig. 79)
SHANBALLY CASTLE
Shanbally Demesne
(c. 1812)

This, the largest of John Nash's castellated houses, was built for Cornelius O'Callaghan, first Viscount Lismore. It was demolished in 1957 and the ruin dynamited. A gate lodge of 1914 and some outbuildings are all that remain.

(fig. 80)
BIANCONI MORTUARY CHAPEL
Ardmayle East
(1857)

Charles Bianconi designed this mausoleum, in the village of Boherlahan, in the Italianate style of his homeland. The chapel is dedicated to St Catherine and contains an effigy of Bianconi by Belzoni.

reflected on the façade. In 1954, the Land Commission purchased the estate and, as with many other demesnes, constructed roads across it to facilitate its subdivision. The castle stood empty until 1957 when it was needlessly destroyed. The roof and the cut stone were removed, and explosives were used to destroy much of what remained. ***(fig. 79)***.

In 1846 Charles Bianconi purchased Longfield House, near Cashel. He brought specialist gardeners from Italy to enhance its setting and planted a rose garden, with white and yellow roses to represent the Joyful and Glorious Mysteries of the Rosary, and red roses to represent the Sorrowful Mysteries. His mausoleum at Boherlahan, built in 1857, is a fitting memorial to this most enterprising of men ***(fig. 80)***.

Changing tastes in architecture among the gentry in the early nineteenth century led to the construction or renovation of country houses in a variety of styles. Coolville House, Clogheen, built in 1804 by the Grubb family, alongside their flour-mill complex, is a more typical and restrained house of the period ***(fig. 81)***. Newtownanner House, near Clonmel, has fine decorative details and was largely constructed in 1829 ***(figs. 82-3)***. Some of the wealthier population chose to break from the constraints of classical architecture in the design of their stately piles. In many cases earlier houses were refaced or remodelled to reflect newer, fashionable styles. Thomastown Castle

(fig. 81)
COOLVILLE HOUSE
Lower Main Street, Clogheen
(c. 1805)

A branch of the Quaker Grubb family established mills at Clogheen in the eighteenth century. The adjacent mill owner's house is adorned by its fine doorcase with sidelights and a cobweb fanlight. The recessed block was added c. 1885.

(fig. 82)
NEWTOWNANNER HOUSE
Newtownanner Demesne
(1829)

The seat of the Osborne family at Newtownanner has an unusual plan, the middle bays being lower than the projecting ends. Its entrance door case displays a particularly elaborate fanlight. The house is set in extensive landscaped grounds with a lake, canal, recently restored temple, gardener's house, a very fine stable block and important specimen trees.

NEWTOWNANNER HOUSE

(fig. 83)
THE TEMPLE WATER
Newtownanner Demesne
(c. 1830)

Classical temples on the shores of artificial lakes were a common feature of eighteenth and nineteenth-century country house demesnes. This scene was photographed c. 1860 by the noted local photographer, Dr William Hemphill.

was refaced in 1812, to the design of Richard Morrison, who also added stables and other buildings ***(figs. 84-5)***. The Gothic Revival makeover included the addition of numerous battlements, turrets and towers. In its current ruinous state, these give the building a convincingly antique appearance. Lismacue and Kilcooly Abbey, both originally constructed in the eighteenth century, were remodelled in the nineteenth century, Lismacue being given a Gothic overcoat, with crenellations on the roof and a porch in limestone ***(figs. 86-7)***. Tullamain Castle, designed by the self-educated and prolific local architect William Tinsley (1804-85) and completed in 1835, is another 'romantic castle' that remains in use as a family residence. Tinsley was also responsible for the design of

(fig. 84)
THOMASTOWN CASTLE
Thomastown Demesne
(Remodelled 1812)

George Mathew, half-brother of the Great Duke of Ormond, built a house here c. 1670. It was enlarged c. 1711 by his grandson, also George, and again in 1812 by his descendant Francis, Second Earl of Llandaff. Francis engaged Richard Morrison to design a castellated mansion, an idea fashionable at the time and incorporating Gothic turrets, crenellations and with hood-mouldings to the windows. The building fell into disuse when it changed hands in the 1870s, and today forms a spectacular ruin.

(fig. 85)
THOMASTOWN CASTLE

This gateway is one of the more intact parts of the site and displays many of the features added to the house in the early nineteenth century.

(fig. 86)
LISMACUE HOUSE
Lismacue
(Remodelled 1816)

The south block of Lismacue, at Bansha, dates to c. 1760, the building being extended in 1816 and the ornate Gothic façades applied. The entrance bay is framed in cut limestone and sandstone with decorative shield devices to the parapet. The use of blind window openings is curious and the stonework of the lower service block to the north, although sharing many of the details of the main house, is left unrendered.

(fig. 87)
KILCOOLY ABBEY
Kilcoolyabbey
(1764, rebuilt 1842)

This substantial country house, set in a large demesne near Urlingford and adjacent to the medieval Cistercian abbey of Kilcooly, is substantially the rebuilding of Sir William Barker's house of 1764, which had been destroyed by fire.

(fig. 88)
LAKEFIELD
Ballygambon
(1831)

William Tinsley, the renowned local architect, designed this late Georgian country house near Fethard for William Pennefather. The façade has a strong horizontal emphasis, capped by a wide over-hanging roof.

(fig. 89)
SUMMERHILL HOUSE
Summerhill
(c. 1820)

The gate piers at Summerhill, near Clonmel, are adorned with carved pineapples.

SUNVILLE
Ardgeeha Lower/Burgagery-Lands West
(c. 1900)

These gates display high quality metal-casting and stone-cutting.

several smaller classical houses in the county. Lakefield, which he designed for the Pennefather family in 1831, is an elegant Italian Renaissance villa, with wide eaves, a Wyatt (tripartite) window above a Doric portico and curved sweeps enclosing a walled garden ***(fig. 88)***. Grove House, near Fethard, was also extended by Tinsley and landscaping works carried out c.1830. Many properties were also provided with notable entrance gateways ***(fig. 89)***.

It has been noted that the design of estate landscapes in the nineteenth century owed much to the idealisation of rustic life, in which the realities of living on the land and of agricultural production were concealed from polite view. In the context of South Tipperary, the disparity between the conditions affecting the small landowner and tenant farmer and those of the landowners, some of who commissioned these expensive demesne landscapes, provided the driving force behind the continuing unrest in South Tipperary throughout the century. The struggle for land reform had ethnic and religious underpinnings, despite the prominence of Protestant leaders, such as Isaac Butt and Charles Stewart Parnell in the Home Rule party and in the Land League. The Land Act of 1881, which provided fixity of tenure, fair rent and free sale of land, central issues in the land agitation, proved to be just a staging-post. In the Plan of Campaign, begun in 1886 to agitate for the lowering of rents, one of the principal targets was the Smith-Barry estate at Tipperary. The scale of resistance associated with the Plan of Campaign is visible in the construction of the suburb of New Tipperary in 1890, sponsored by the Tenants Defence Association ***(fig. 90)***. The houses were occupied by tenants who had been evicted as a result of the agitation, or who had abandoned premises rented from Smith-Barry in the town centre. The venture was not a success and few houses remain in their original form, although 9 Emmet Street, restored in 1990, is an example.

Despite changing tastes, designs for the middle-sized country house remained similar to

(fig. 90)
O'BRIEN ARCADE
Tipperary
(1890)

This arcade, named after the local Nationalist MP, was erected as part of an integrated urban scheme, built in response to popular agitation against the local Smith-Barry estate. It provided premises for shopkeepers evicted for non-payment of rent and also acted as a focus for an enterprise which led to the construction of a whole new residential quarter at the west side of the town.

(fig. 91)
KILMURRY LODGE
Ballynamona
(Kilmurry par.)
(c. 1830)

This is a rare example in South Tipperary of a villa-type house. It is enhanced by the elegant steps to the projecting entrance bay and the string course between the piano nobile and the basement. It is located near Ballyneill.

(fig. 92)
MOUNTAIN LODGE
Cullenagh
(Shanrahan par.)
(c. 1830)

Built by the Butlers as a hunting lodge, Mountain Lodge is distinguished by an irregular footprint and some very fine detailing. A delicate wrought-iron valence graces the eaves. The openings have carved limestone label-mouldings, that to the doorway being stopped with lions' heads, a conceit on the nature of the local game.

those of the late eighteenth century. While one can note an increase in the size of windows - as much a result of the availability of larger panes of glass, as a matter of taste - the basic two- or three-storey house retained its classical proportions. Similarly, in the smaller single-storey-over-half-basement houses, the classical idiom was retained, although expression of individual taste is sometimes to be seen in details such as the treatment of the principal doorway ***(fig. 91)***. Most, however, are unadorned. Mountain Lodge, near Cahir, was built c.1830 as a hunting lodge in a cottage orné style ***(fig. 92)***.

Modest single-storey vernacular houses, with farm buildings ranged around a yard, were built throughout the first half of the century. Most have been extended over time and their original thatched roof-coverings replaced with slate or corrugated iron ***(figs. 93-4)***. In South Tipperary, water reed is the most common thatching material, but there is evidence that

(fig. 93)
BALLYDUGGAN
(c. 1800)

The traditional irregularity of fenestration is seen in this rural thatched house near Ninemilehouse. Its steeply-pitched thatched roof and shallow windbreak are also typical.

(fig. 94)
NOAN
(c. 1800)

Relatively few vernacular houses remain thatched today. Slate has replaced thatch in many instances. This house at Ballinure has simple but attractive detailing.

(fig. 95)
MOORSTOWN
(c. 1850)

Intact two-storey vernacular houses, like this one near Cahir, are relatively rare. They share the traditional plan and layout of the smaller houses. The chimneystack and entrance of this farmhouse betray a lobby-entry layout.

cereal straw was formerly predominant. As the century advanced, larger, two-storey houses were built, usually with pitched slate roofs ***(fig. 95)***. The builders of some vernacular houses have opted for fairly symmetrical front elevations and regular fenestration, showing a degree of classical influence on the vernacular tradition. The majority of farm buildings are single-storey and have corrugated-iron roofs, although there are also two-storey slate-roofed examples ***(fig. 96)***. At Monslatt, near Killenaule, is a very rare round-plan thatched outbuilding, with a conical roof ***(fig. 97)***.

(fig. 96)
MURGASTY
(c. 1800)

This well-maintained out-building stands in the small farmyard of a thatched house just outside Tipperary Town.

(fig. 97)
MONSLATT
(c. 1800)

Thatched farm buildings are now extremely rare in the eastern half of Ireland. This round-plan outhouse near Killenaule is possibly unique.

(fig. 98)
MAIN GUARD
Sarsfield Street/
Mitchell Street,
Clonmel
(1675, remodelled
c. 1810)

Prior to recent conservation and restoration of its seventeenth-century arcaded form, the Main Guard's ground floor housed three traditional shopfronts with two inserted floors above. The assembly was somewhat at odds with the heavy moulded cornices and pediment, and the armorial plaques to the first floor which testified to its high status in the town.

OLDBRIDGE
(1843)

A cast-iron plaque marking the boundary of the borough of Clonmel.

(fig. 99)
WEST GATE
O'Connell Street/
Irishtown,
Clonmel
(1831)

This gateway, on the site of the medieval west gate of the walled town, provides a counterpoint to the Main Guard at the opposite end of O'Connell Street. It was erected on the initiative of a local merchant, a Mr Joyce, in a Tudor Revival style.

WEST GATE

Detail of the west elevation.

The established urban structure of South Tipperary, dating from Anglo-Norman times, maintained and increased its importance through the nineteenth century. Unlike other parts of Ireland, South Tipperary has few examples of core settlements associated with its landed estates. In general, pre-existing towns became the economic and administrative centres. Many also had garrisons, reflecting the tensions for which the county became notorious in the nineteenth century.

Despite the uncertainties and tensions of the time, the greater ease of travel and transport stimulated the growth of towns, generating the construction of new commercial, religious and institutional structures. As the value of property rose, the propensity for adaptation seen in the country houses was manifested in the towns, but with an entirely utilitarian motivation. In Clonmel, the seventeenth-century courthouse of the Tipperary Palatinate was extensively altered, with floors inserted, to accommodate shops with dwellings above ***(fig. 98)***. At the same time, the street line behind the building was brought forward to create additional commercial space, while the square in front of the building was partly built over. The fashion for the medieval, expressed in the reworking of country houses in the Gothic style, is visible in the reconstruction of the West Gate in 1831 ***(fig. 99)***. In Fethard, the conventual buildings of the medieval Augustinian Friary were partly converted - the east range used for storage and the south range demolished and a mill built on part of the site. The friary returned to the Augustinians in 1820 and was restored for religious services, the medieval tower being taken down in 1836 and a new west front and entrance doorway being added, with a gallery above ***(fig. 100)***.

(fig. 100)
FETHARD AUGUSTINIAN ABBEY
Abbeyville,
Fethard
(remodelled 1836)

The picture shows the abbey church, with its roofless transept. In the background is the late eighteenth-century corn mill, built on the site of part of the south range. A new entrance façade was built in 1836 in Gothic style, incorporating stones from the medieval tower then recently taken down.

(fig. 101)
JOHN STREET
Cashel
(c. 1830)

This street, leading up to the Church of Ireland cathedral, is lined with fine two and three-storey town houses, some incorporating carriage entrances. A large petal fanlight dominates the wide entrance doorway of this example. The fenestration pattern is carried through to the neighbouring house and the steps, protruding into the footpath, help to emphasise the position of the entrance at the centre of the façade.

(fig. 102)
O'CONNOR BROS
35-36 Main Street,
Tipperary
(c. 1800)

O'Connor Bros has a classic render and timber shopfront in a town which has the best collection of traditional shopfronts in the county. The upper floors are accessed by the doorway at the left. The decorative detailing is typical of the high quality of render and other details in Tipperary Town.

(fig. 103)
22-25 GLADSTONE STREET
Clonmel
(c. 1840)

A terrace of substantial town houses of three storeys over basements with elaborate limestone doorcases and cast-iron railings.

In the town cores, the vibrant class of merchants and traders built new two-, three- or four-storey premises for their businesses. Their dwellings, as in John Street in Cashel, often incorporated carriage arches in their front façades ***(fig. 101)***. Tipperary Town has many fine examples of nineteenth-century commercial buildings, particularly on Main Street. The premises of O'Connor Brothers (c.1800), illustrates the type: ground-floor shop, with a separate access to the residence in the floors above ***(fig. 102)***. The streetscapes produced by the juxtaposition of such buildings display the variety and inventiveness of detail typical of market towns in the nineteenth century. O'Connell Street and Gladstone Street in Clonmel and Main Street in Cashel provide other good examples ***(figs. 103-5)***. However, the towns of Cahir and Tipperary have the most distinctive and unified architectural characters. In Cahir, William Tinsley is credited with the redesign of Castle Street and The Square. The resulting streetscapes are most attractive and buildings have common detailing, particularly in the use

FRIAR STREET,
Cashel
c. 1880

(fig. 104)
M. RYAN
76 Main Street,
Cashel
(c. 1870)

Shallow Ionic-style pilasters adorn the rendered frontage of this public house.

(fig. 105)
M. RYAN

The interior is still very traditional.

(fig. 106)
THE SQUARE
Cahir
(c. 1840)

William Tinsley was engaged by the Earl of Glengall to remodel much of the town of Cahir. This resulted in the consistent treatment of façades, especially on the north side of Castle Street and the west side of The Square. His hallmark is the distinctive use of gabled, panelled pilasters in ashlar sandstone. The leftmost pilasters are replacements for three lost by the late nineteenth century.

(fig. 107)
KENNEDY
The Square,
Cahir
(c. 1840)

This shopfront has cut sandstone pilasters and a marble stall riser inscribed with the proprietor's name.

W.J. IRWIN
The Square,
Cahir
(c. 1840)

Detail of gabled pilaster.

(fig. 108)
CASTLE STREET
Cahir
(c. 1860)

This three-light oriel window ornately punctuates the streetscape opposite Cahir Castle.

of label-mouldings over the windows and of cut-sandstone shopfronts, giving the town a particularly unified architectural character ***(figs. 106-7)***. Decorative oriel windows are a feature of Castle Street ***(fig. 108)***. Tipperary Town has a large number of fine shop fronts, mainly of the second half of the century. High quality classical detailing is a particular feature of the town, in the form of triple-arched ground floors to many buildings, the divisions being made by marble columns with skilfully crafted capitals ***(fig. 109)***. Columns are also visible as mullions to double-windows to some upper floors. More modest shopfronts can be found in some of the smaller towns ***(fig. 110)***.

(fig. 109)
THE AULD MURRAY
Main Street,
Tipperary Town
(c. 1870)

One of the most characteristic features of the remarkably unified street architecture of Tipperary Town is the use of arcaded ground floors. In this instance, Corinthian polished granite colonettes separate the windows and the cornice has courses of modillions, and egg-and-dart and leaf motifs.

THE AULD MURRAY

BRUDAIR'S BAKERY
Main Street,
Tipperary Town
(c. 1880)

Marble columns divide the upper floor windows of many buildings on Tipperary's Main Street.

(fiG. 110)
FITZGIBBON
Main Street/
Chapel Street,
Cappawhite
(c. 1860)

Fitzgibbon's public house has good render detailing in its fluted pilasters, moulded and dentillated cornice and applied lettering.

OLD QUAY
Clonmel
c. 1880

This view of the quayside in Clonmel has changed radically since the late nineteenth century. Only Old Bridge and part of the mill buildings to the left have survived. The tower of St Mary's Catholic Church, Irishtown, can be seen in the distance. The buildings in the foreground had the slate cladding so distinctive of the town.

(fig. 111)
GOVERNMENT OFFICES
New Quay/
Nelson Street,
Clonmel
(c. 1830)

Castellated parapets adorn the roofline of this large former brewery building on the quayside in Clonmel. It was the premises of Thomas Murphy & Co. and the complex covered an area of about two acres. Its original main building was constructed in 1798, but was rebuilt after a fire in 1829. It later served as a shoe and boot factory.

The continuing significance of the grain trade is seen in the changes made to the quays in Clonmel. In the seventeenth century, the town had four corn-mills and a mill for wool, but from the mid-eighteenth century this activity greatly expanded. The old quay had been sufficient up to then, but over the next twenty years the quay walls were levelled and an embankment constructed. In 1840 over the county generally, there were between 60 and 70 mills: Clonmel and its environs had no fewer than 120 millstones in operation, as well as breweries and other industries ***(fig. 111)***. The mills in Cahir are unique in that they were part of an initiative of the Earl of Glengall to stimulate the economy of his estates. The scale and extent of the milling industry at its peak may be gleaned from the complex of country house, mill, millers' houses and ancillary buildings at Castlegrace, near Clogheen ***(fig. 112)***. The vast mill building, dating from the turn of the nineteenth century, is disused but remains substantially intact ***(see fig. 48)***.

(fig. 112)
CASTLEGRACE
(c. 1800)

Symmetrically placed millers' houses flank the approach to the mills at Castlegrace. The house to the right has a single-storey front and a two-storey rear elevation and was the bank for the enterprise.

(fig. 113)
CLONMEL ARMS HOTEL
Sarsfield Street,
Clonmel
(c. 1845)

The former Trustee Savings Bank was designed with fine classical detailing. It stands on Sarsfield Street, a thoroughfare that is particularly rich in historic buildings.

(fig. 114)
AIB BANK
Lower Main Street,
Clogheen
(c. 1875)

The plan and detailing of this bank building would be more usual for a dwelling house. The projecting gable, with its group of pointed windows, is almost convent-like. The building is attributed to the office of Deane and Woodward.

(fig. 115)
BANK OF IRELAND
Parnell Street/
Nelson Street,
Clonmel
(c. 1860)

The Italianate palazzo style was very popular in the second half of the nineteenth century for financial institutions. The county town's former National Bank has appropriately classical detailing, enhanced by its prominent corner site close to the town hall and courthouse.

The increasing importance of the towns in the commercial life of the region was expressed in the new bank buildings. Many were notable features of the main streets as well as being considerable works in themselves. Sadlier's Bank was established in Tipperary Town in 1803 as a private bank, originally located in the mid-eighteenth-century Georgian town house of James Scully, a wealthy farmer. It collapsed after 1856 and in 1866 the bank building became the Clanwilliam Club. Purpose-built bank buildings were constructed in virtually every town, generally in a restrained version of classicism, and were both places of business and dwellings ***(figs. 113-4)***. The Bank of Ireland in Clonmel is a particularly fine example ***(fig. 115)***.

(fig. 116)
1-24 ANNE STREET
Clonmel
(1821)

Thomas Tinsley, father of William, designed this exquisite street of twenty-four houses opposite the western approach to St Mary's Church of Ireland church. The houses are skilfully designed, their elegant proportions disguising their height.

(fig. 117)
9 ANNE STREET

This house has a cobweb fanlight characteristic of the street, and a discreet basement opening.

(*fig. 118*)
THE MALL
Cahir
(1825-30)

This fine terrace of three-storey over basement houses stands overlooking the River Suir near Cahir Castle. Originally, the Castle Street end was closed off by a gate.

On streets adjoining the town centres, new terraced housing for the middle classes was constructed, often in a late Georgian style. Exceptional examples can be found in Clonmel and Cahir. Thomas Tinsley, father of William, designed Anne Street, Clonmel in 1821, with its twenty-four three-storey houses ***(figs. 116-7)***. The large houses on The Mall, Cahir, were built between 1825 and 1830 and form a most elegant assembly of buildings in a riverside setting ***(fig. 118)***. The houses on New Quay, Clonmel are of three storeys over a basement and were built in 1830. They have had to contend with the vagaries of the River Suir and its tendency to overflow its channel within the town ***(fig. 119)***. Dr Croke Place has a terrace of ten two-storey houses with attics, designed by William Tinsley in 1842 at the behest of the Grubb family ***(fig. 120)***. Detached houses were also constructed on the urban fringes, such as Alta Villa (1820) in Cahir and plentifully in Clonmel, built mainly for Quaker merchant

(*fig. 119*)
3 NEW QUAY
Clonmel
(c. 1805)

The quayside at Clonmel is notable for its merchants' houses whose main floors are raised above understoreys to protect against flooding and are similar to houses on South Mall, Cork. This house is one of a mirror-image pair, with elegant Doric doorcases.

4 NEW QUAY
Clonmel
(c. 1805)

This carved limestone doorcase is skilfully crafted with Classical detailing.

(fig. 120)
1-10 DOCTOR CROKE PLACE
Clonmel
(1842)

William Tinsley designed this terrace of ten houses, formerly called Regent's Terrace, for the Grubb family of industrialists. They are distinguished by their concave doorways and fine fanlights.

(fig. 121)
MINELLA HOTEL
Coleville Road, Clonmel
(1863)

The bowed garden elevation of Minella, a house designed by J.S. Mulvany for the wealthy Quaker milling family of Malcolmson.

(fig. 122)
LORETO CONVENT
Coleville Road,
Clonmel
(c. 1840)

William Tinsley designed this house for the Murray family. It is adorned by gables, projecting windows and an elegant carved timber porch.

ASHBOURNE
Coleville Road,
Clonmel
(c. 1840)

This house was designed by William Tinsley for the wealthy Davis family. It shows the decorative detailing and the irregularity of form typical of the time.

families. Melview (1835) and Minella (1863) were both designed by J.S. Mulvany for the Malcolmsons and Loreto and Ashbourne were designed c.1840 by William Tinsley for the Murray and Davis families ***(figs. 121-2)*** . They all demonstrate the variety of style in domestic building that characterised the nineteenth century as it unfolded. In the latter part of the century development of the urban edges, with the construction of detached and semi-detached houses in their own gardens, became commonplace.

(fig. 123)
AHENNY
(c. 1870)

These former slate quarry workers' houses are ranged in terraces along three streets in an otherwise rural setting. The ensemble is a smaller version of the industrial village at Portlaw, Co. Waterford.

A significant feature of the time was the construction of housing for the artisans and labourers associated with industrial and commercial enterprises as well as with estates, and built in a style that echoed that of the principal buildings. The process was aided by the availability of pattern books providing a range of options for the intending builder. The slate-workers' houses in Ahenny are small single-storey buildings in a neo-vernacular idiom, contrasting with the workers' housing associated with Gould's Cross railway station and the estate workers' houses at Knocklofty, carefully designed as part of a larger context ***(figs. 123-4)***. Throughout the country the 1890s saw the construction, on a wide scale, of labourers' cottages, an undertaking that was to become increasingly the task of the local authorities in the twentieth century. The former King Street flats in Clonmel, built by the military, in 1878 as married quarters and upgraded recently as social housing, present a much larger scale and architectural ambition ***(fig. 125)***. Other public works include the fine collection of fountains in the towns of Cahir, Cashel and Tipperary ***(figs. 126-7)***.

One of the distinguishing features of the nineteenth-century town is the appearance of institutional buildings - structures specifically

(fig. 124)
MONKSLAND
(c. 1880)

These small semi-detached houses have all the decorative details associated with estate workers' houses. They were built on the estate of the nearby Knocklofty House.

(fig. 125)
ST FRANCIS' COURT
King Street,
Clonmel
(1878)

This H-plan former barracks accommodation block was built in 1878 and recently upgraded with the addition of access galleries.

(fig. 126)
BACK OF THE PIPES
Main Street,
Cashel
(1842)

The Town Commissioners erected this limestone reservoir in 1842 to provide a water supply for the townspeople. The spouts have decorative lions' heads.

(fig. 127)
BUTLER CHARTERIS
FOUNTAIN
The Square,
Cahir
(1876)

Lady Margaret Charteris of Cahir Park contributed this carved sandstone fountain to the people of Cahir in memory of her husband, Richard. Possibly designed by Sir Charles Lanyon, it displays a mixture of medieval and nineteenth-century motifs.

(fig. 128)
CLONOULTY
CHURCHQUARTER
(c. 1830)

The four leftmost bays appear to have been the original school building, with separate entrances at each end of the façade for girls and boys. The school was extended southwards in a sympathetic way in the late twentieth century, to accommodate increased demand.

designed to fulfil military, religious, educational or social purposes. Many reflected wider reforms: the National Board of Education, formed in 1806, initiated a comprehensive system of education for children, and the provision of school buildings was gradually extended, under the patronage of the churches and local landlords. However, the educational landscape also witnessed a struggle along confessional lines, with several evangelical societies regarding education as the principal means of weaning the majority population away from the 'errors of Papism'. The early years of the century saw an increase in the numbers of both parochial and private schools, built in a variety of styles. Early rural examples often consisted of a single room heated with an open fire, and lit by large windows. Estate schools tended to be formal in style, akin to minor estate buildings such as lodges. The national school (1830) at Clonoulty demonstrates how quickly the building type developed ***(fig. 128)***. Other schools of architectural interest from the period include the Erasmus Smith School (1818) in Cahir by John Nash, the Free School in Clonmel (1826), built to a design by the Pain Brothers, and the Model School (1848) also in Clonmel, designed by Frederick Darley ***(figs. 129-30)***. The Abbey Grammar School at Tipperary was rebuilt in 1820 ***(fig. 131)***. The well-preserved Curraghpoor National School, near Donaskeagh, was built in 1891 and has

(fig. 129)
ERASMUS SMITH BUILDING
Church Street,
Cahir
(1818)

A schoolhouse designed by the noted architect John Nash, this building forms part of a setting with the nearby St Paul's Church of Ireland church. It has similar detailing, especially evident in the pinnacles, and the castellations and turrets echo the architecture of Cahir Castle. It was envisaged as a multi-denominational establishment. It is now used as local authority offices.

(fig. 130)
MODEL SCHOOL
Western Road,
Clonmel
(1848)

Frederick Darley was responsible for the Tudor Revival style of this former school. It has a complex plan and fine limestone details. The front garden and cast-iron railings contribute to its pleasant and dignified setting.

(fig. 131)
ABBEY SCHOOL
Abbey Street/
Railway Road,
Tipperary
(1820)

A new school was built in 1955 on much of the site of the school designed in 1820 by Thomas Coleborne, a partner of the well-known architect Francis Johnston. Erasmus Smith had founded a grammar school here in 1669 under a charter of Charles II. An Act of 1938 transferred the school to the State, since which time it has been run by the Christian Brothers. The arch to the left of the school building was the last upstanding part of the medieval Augustinian abbey. It was demolished in the 1955 works.

(fig. 132)
CURRAGHPOOR
NATIONAL SCHOOL
Gorteen
(Rathlynin par.)
(1891)

This relatively large rural national school retains its original character and details. The porch is an addition of 1930.

(fig. 133)
PARISH PASTORAL CENTRE
Friar Street,
Cashel
(1860)

This former female national school was built by the Presentation nuns and forms a pleasant streetscape boundary for their convent complex. The ground floor windows have decorative vents to their upper sashes. The elaborate middle gates lead into the forecourt of St John the Baptist Catholic Church.

several plaques marking the various phases of construction ***(fig. 132)***. The increasing role of the State in education as the century progressed, was reflected in the more standardised school designs of the Office of Public Works. Larger establishments, such as the school and convent complex in Cashel, dating from 1830, became important elements of the urban landscape as the century advanced ***(fig. 133)***.

As the administrative centre of the county, Clonmel experienced exceptional growth at the beginning of the century. Its administrative

(fig. 134)
CLONMEL COURTHOUSE
Nelson Street,
Clonmel
(c. 1800)

Richard Morrison is credited with the courthouse in Clonmel, which has fine sandstone detailing to its principal elevation. The pedimented entrance arcade is a suitably monumental introduction to this judicial building. The six-bay rear elevation has a low-pitch pediment to the middle four bays, with wings at right angles to each side, and typically, round-headed windows to the first floor. The courthouse was the scene of the trial of William Smith O'Brien and his co-conspirators in the abortive rebellion of 1848.

(fig. 135)
CLONMEL COURTHOUSE

The vestibule.

importance is reflected in a range of public buildings. In about 1800 a new courthouse was built, designed by Richard Morrison ***(figs. 134-5)***. It is a neo-Palladian building with a central three-bay pedimented breakfront. In plan, it resembles James Gandon's courthouse in Waterford, with its twin stairs rising from the entrance hall. A town hall was constructed in 1881, just outside the medieval town wall, on the site of a seventeenth-century mansion built by Richard Hamerton, which had become the Globe Inn in the eighteenth century ***(fig. 136)***. The former town hall in Cashel has fine architectural

(fig. 136)
CLONMEL TOWN HALL
Parnell Street,
Clonmel
(1881)

The town house of Richard Hamerton stood on this site in the late seventeenth century, to be succeeded by the Great Globe Inn in the following century. In 1881, during the mayoralty of Edward Cantwell, the building was reconstructed as a town hall, in what has been described as a jolly Flemish Renaissance style. The statue outside commemorates the rebels of the 1798 rising. It was sculpted by James K. Bracken and unveiled in 1904.

detailing and stands proudly in the centre of the medieval marketplace ***(fig. 137)***. The former town hall in Cahir had its ground floor broken out in the twentieth century. Elsewhere in the county, courthouses were built with modest architectural ambitions: those at Carrick-on-Suir, Clogheen and Tipperary Town use a standard design attributed to William Caldbeck ***(fig. 138)***. All three have five-bay two-storey principal elevations and similar limestone details, such as a plat band between the floors, a moulded cornice and pediments over the paired doorways. The building in Tipperary Town (1839) was built by J.K. Fahie and has a return block to give a T-plan. Wherever courts

(fig. 137)
CASHEL TOURIST OFFICE
Main Street,
Cashel
(1866)

The former City Hall in Cashel, designed by J.E. Rogers in an interpretation of the Romanesque style, has two principal elevations: its front and its west gable–the rear elevation is surprisingly plain and irregular. The ground floor arcade indicates the former function of the building as a market house. The arcade motif continues to the first floor windows of the gable. An armorial plaque of 1631, from an earlier building on the site or elsewhere in the town, is set into the doorway over the lower annex.

(fig. 138)
CLOGHEEN COURTHOUSE
Barrack Hill,
Clogheen
(1841)

Its curious location on a narrow site is the reason for the painted short façade, rather than the entrance elevation, of this courthouse facing the street. A plaque on the building names Cornelius O'Callaghan as foreman and Samuel Jones, County Surveyor, as the engineer.

(fig. 139)
CARRIGEEN CASTLE
Mitchelstown Road, Cahir
(1812-16, enlarged 1849-50)

This former bridewell for the town of Cahir closed in 1878 and was used as a military officers' residence until 1919, since when it has been a dwelling.

were established, gaols and bridewells were also to be found. Several bridewells were built in the county, as places of detention catering for minor offences, such as drunkenness. They also functioned as the equivalent of today's remand centres. The Cahir bridewell (1819), possibly by the architect Michael Bernard Mullins, is now known as Carrigeen Castle and apparently incorporates the fabric of a military fort of c. 1600. Extended in 1850, the building is an irregular three-storey castellated structure that had eight cells, two dayrooms, six keeper's rooms and two exercise yards. It was closed in 1878, becoming quarters for military officers until 1919, since when it has been a dwelling house ***(fig. 139)***. The bridewell in Tipperary Town was built in the early 1840s, and had sixteen cells, four of them for females. It was used as a gaol after the Fenian revolt of 1867, closed in 1886 following a countrywide rationalisation of bridewells, but re-opened in 1922, during the Civil War, to hold Republican prisoners.

While military barracks were a feature of the major towns since the end of the Cromwellian wars, the nineteenth century witnessed the construction of several purpose-built establishments. The first such complex, in Clonmel, had been constructed in 1780, being replaced in 1805 by the present Kickham Barracks ***(figs. 140-1)***. Only the boundary wall now survives of the vast barracks that stood to the south of Cahir. In 1876, the garrison in Tipperary Town was accommodated in a complex located opposite the workhouse ***(fig. 142)***. Clonmel also had substantial blocks built in 1860 for the South Tipperary Militia, on Emmet

(fig. 140)
KICKHAM BARRACKS
Davis Road,
Clonmel
(c. 1830)

The barracks at Clonmel was begun c. 1805. The main building is the Officers' Mess of c. 1830, built in the style of a country house with a pediment and wings connected to the main block by lower arcaded links.

(fig. 141)
PRIVATES' MESS
Kickham Barracks,
Davis Road,
Clonmel
(1876)

The Privates' Mess and a number of other key buildings were erected in 1876 and have consistent, good quality construction, with a playful colourful and textural contrast of materials. There is snecked sandstone for the walls, dressed limestone for the eaves, quoins, plinths and lintels, and brick for the jambs of doors and windows.

PRIVATES' MESS

Street, one building now housing the Garda Síochána and another being greatly modified in 1927 to become the headquarters of South Tipperary County Council ***(fig. 143)***. The former police barracks at Tipperary is also an impressive structure ***(fig. 144)***. Small constabulary barracks were constructed in rural areas and in smaller settlements, such as New Inn, Dundrum and at Mealclye, near Annacarty ***(figs. 145-6)***.

The Poor Relief (Ireland) Act in 1838 established workhouses to accommodate 'paupers', those destitute people for whom it constituted a last resort. Poorhouses and almshouses were

(fig. 142)
TIPPERARY MILITARY BARRACKS
Station Road, Tipperary
(c. 1880)

An unusual and well-built limestone water tower is the only building still standing within the boundary walls of the former military barracks at Tipperary.

(fig. 143)
CLONMEL GARDA STATION
Emmet Street, Clonmel
(c. 1875)

Originally built c. 1875, as part of the Victoria Militia Barracks, this building became a Garda station in 1926. A surprisingly light effect is achieved by the wide spacing of the windows and the hanging detail to the eaves.

(fig. 144)
TIPPERARY RIC BARRACKS
Davis Street/ St Michael's Road, Tipperary
(c. 1875)

Built in the same year as the militia barracks in Clonmel, the RIC barracks at Tipperary has a more fortress-like appearance, emphasised by its H-plan and the stepped access to the main floor of the building. It has similarities to barracks at Bruff and Pallasgrean, Co. Limerick.

(fig. 145)
DUNDRUM GARDA STATION
Garryduff East
(c. 1865)

Tudor Revival style and detailing are evident in this distinctive former RIC barracks. It was built under the influence of the Hawardens of Dundrum House, as part of what has been described as a 'carefully contrived alien cell with its inn, courthouse, Anglican church, corn mill and constabulary barracks'.

DUNDRUM GARDA STATION

Detail of an entrance projection, with protective slit openings to the doorway.

(fig. 146)
MEALCLYE
(c. 1820)

An unusual form for a police barracks, this building provided the model for a series of similar structures around Ireland. Its design is loosely based on the medieval tower house. The barracks was burned out during the Civil War.

in existence since at least the time of the monasteries, and the workhouse system was financed through a property tax, called the 'poor rate'. The buildings, of various scales, were based on standardised layouts, devised by George Wilkinson, featuring separate male and female accommodation. The good quality of the design and construction of many of these buildings should be acknowledged, despite their dismal place in the folk memory of Irish people. Wilkinson generally favoured a simplified Tudor style, the complex in Cashel, built in 1842 with later additions, being an example. The Tipperary workhouse opened the same year and served the west of the county, as well as east Limerick ***(fig. 147)***. In the later years of the Great Famine, as earlier efforts at providing relief through work were seen to fail, workhouses became notorious for high mortality rates among their overcrowded occupants. In 1850 alone, over 1200 people died in the Tipperary workhouse, 60 per cent of them children.

As the numbers in the workhouses declined in the years after the Famine, workhouse hospitals became significant medical institutions. The Sisters of Mercy began nursing in the Tipperary workhouse hospital in 1874. Hospitals developed systematically through the nineteenth century, as more informed attitudes to health and advances in hygiene led to the construction of purpose-built, sometimes specialised, hospital buildings. St Luke's Mental Hospital (1833), designed in the manner of Francis Johnston's institutional buildings, stands part way up the prominent ridge overlooking the north side of Clonmel ***(fig. 148)***. On the adjoining site to the east is St Joseph's Hospital (1855), now South Tipperary General Hospital.

Many of the rural Protestant churches of the late eighteenth and early nineteenth century were constructed on earlier ecclesiastical sites. The church at Marlfield in First Fruits style, designed by Thomas Tinsley and built in 1818,

(fig. 147)
TIPPERARY WORKHOUSE
Station Road,
Tipperary
(1841)

Tipperary's workhouse is largely intact and is considerably enhanced by the quality of its limestone detailing, particularly evident in its Tudor-arch doorways. The entrance block, viewed here, stands between the usual taller and projecting end wings.

(fig. 148)
ST LUKE'S HOSPITAL
Western Road,
Clonmel
(1833)

The former mental hospital at Clonmel was influenced by the work of Francis Johnston and is similar to that in Waterford City. Of good quality limestone work, the long horizontal composition is given added interest by its louvered 'top knot' or tower, which has a date of 1833 inscribed in Roman numerals to the base.

ST LUKE'S HOSPITAL

is at the site of the Cistercian monastery of Inishlounaght and its builders have reused some of the features of the nearby abbey ***(fig. 149)***. This church could be seen to reflect in its fabric the overturning of the old order and its replacement by the new: a process that was the defining characteristic of developments throughout the century in South Tipperary. Ardmayle Church of Ireland church also incorporates the tower of a medieval church ***(fig. 150)***. Kilcooly has a large First Fruits church built of limestone, with a large west tower ***(fig. 151)***. The churches at Killaloan, near Clonmel, and Magorban, near Cashel are examples of smaller undertakings ***(fig. 152)***. Several fine Protestant churches of this period were built, the most notable being St Paul's, Cahir (1816-18), the only Irish church designed by

(fig. 149)
ST PATRICK'S CHURCH OF IRELAND CHURCH
Marlfield
(1818)

Marlfield church stands on or near the site of the Cistercian abbey of Inishlounaght. It incorporates two surviving elements of the ancient buildings: the traceried east window, and a fine carved doorway repositioned high up on an interior wall.

(fig. 150)
ST JOHN'S CHURCH OF IRELAND CHURCH
Ardmayle
(1814-15)

Ardmayle Church of Ireland is a classic example of a nineteenth-century edifice utilising a pre-existing religious site. The fifteenth-century tower of the medieval church has been incorporated into the later building, whose delicately carved timber windows have trefoil-headed lights.

(fig. 151)
KILCOOLY CHURCH OF IRELAND CHURCH
Kilcoolyabbey
(1829)

This has been described as the finest First Fruits style church in South Tipperary. Its tall west tower is topped with crocketed pinnacles. There were fine traceried timber windows until recent years.

(fig. 152)
CHURCH OF THE HOLY SPIRIT
Magorban
(1813-16)

This Church of Ireland church is the archetypal rural church and graveyard. Its interior evokes a special atmosphere, with a stove for heating, a pump organ for music and candles and oil lamps for lighting, never having been wired for electricity. The ceiling has fine plasterwork details.

MAGORBAN

John Nash. Its soaring spire makes it an important landmark in the town ***(figs. 153-4)***. St Mary's (1830), in Tipperary Town is another fine example of Gothic Revival architecture. The Scots' Church (1844), in Tipperary Town, and the Wesleyan chapel (1843), at Clonmel, were both designed by William Tinsley, the Clonmel building standing on the site of an

(fig. 153)
ST PAUL'S CHURCH
Church Street,
Cahir
(1816-18)

Nash's church at Cahir is one of only two designed by him, the other being All Souls' at Langham Place, London. The front of the Cahir church is unusual, with its entrances flanked by thin spirelets. Gothic detailing is everywhere evident in the building, in the form of turrets, pinnacles, hood-mouldings and traceried windows.

(fig. 154)
ST PAUL'S CHURCH

The plasterwork in St Paul's ceiling incorporates decorative bosses at all intersections of the ribbed vaulting, each displaying a different form of foliage, with a coiled serpent over the crossing. The carved timber pews are rare survivors.

ST PAUL'S CHURCH

earlier one built by his father, Thomas ***(fig. 155)***. These buildings, together with the Quaker Meeting House at Cahir, constructed in 1833 and now a Presbyterian church, are good examples of smaller ecclesiastical buildings in the classical idiom ***(fig. 156)***. The choice of a dignified classicism for these buildings is worth noting, as it has generally been observed that, as the century progressed, Gothic Revival became the idiom of choice for ecclesiastical buildings, and indeed, for a time, for domestic buildings. The Bolton Library at Cashel, a rare example of a freestanding diocesan library, was built in 1836 to house the book collection of Archbishop Theophilus Bolton, as well as providing a chapter house for the Cathedral of St John the Baptist and St Patrick's Rock ***(fig. 157)***.

The re-emergence of the Catholic community found notable expression in the construction of churches. In the early years of the century,

(fig. 155)
WHITE MEMORIAL THEATRE
Wolfe Tone Street, Clonmel
(1843)

The former Wesleyan Methodist church in Clonmel, close to the south entrance of St Mary's Church of Ireland, was designed by William Tinsley in a Greek Revival style. It replaced a chapel of 1804 which had been designed by William's father, Thomas.

(fig. 156)
CAHIR PRESBYTERIAN CHURCH
Abbey Street,
Cahir
(1833)

Built in 1833 and used until 1881 as a Quaker meeting house, the simplicity of this neo-Classical building is elevated by the arched recesses with their fine small-pane timber sliding sash windows. The blind window to the gable is the first view of the building from the street, emphasising the relative modesty of Quaker religious buildings.

(fig. 157)
BOLTON LIBRARY
John Street,
Cashel
(1836)

Archbishop Theophilus Bolton housed his library at his palace on Main Street until a later incumbent erected a purpose-built structure in the grounds of St John the Baptist Cathedral on John Street. The building, with a combination of classical and Georgian elements, houses one of the finest and earliest diocesan libraries in Ireland.

(fig. 158)
ST MARY'S CHURCH
Irishtown,
Clonmel
(1837-80)

Designed by J.B. Keane, St Mary's is a monumental building on the site of a thatched penal chapel. Most of the building is rendered, but an optical illusion is created when one stands directly in front, by the use of ashlar limestone to the gable-front and the forward-facing elevations of the transepts. The portico, with a tower of 1880 and a portico of 1890, has fine classical detailing, the effect heightened by the statues to the pediment.

places of worship for the majority population were usually modest structures, often hidden in back streets of towns or dependent on the goodwill of a landowner for their existence. St Mary's Church Clonmel illustrates the scale and pace of change. It was designed by the architect J.B. Keane and replaced an earlier thatched chapel, through the unusual device of building around the older church, Mass being celebrated in the old and the new on alternate Sundays. The tower was added perhaps by George Goldie c. 1880, and the portico completed ten years later ***(figs. 158-9)***. The Catholic Emancipation Act of 1829 was the watershed, but it was not a sudden and isolated event: amelioration of the Penal Laws had been sporadically introduced from the late eighteenth century, marking the growing involvement of Catholics in the civil and military establishment. The renewed confidence of the Catholic population was expressed in landmark churches around the county, with notable examples in Bansha and Clogheen, as well as in the larger towns of Fethard, Carrick-on-Suir and

(fig. 159)
ST MARY'S CHURCH

The huge internal space has an ornate plaster ceiling, the classical detailing also being carried through in the use of pilasters and the immense Roman Renaissance-style reredos designed by George Goldie in 1867 and inspired by Michelangelo.

Cashel ***(figs. 160-3)***. The Gothic Revival was espoused as the 'true' architecture for Catholic buildings by the English architect A.W.N. Pugin, and his son, E.W. Pugin, the latter in partnership with George Ashlin. This was to have a major influence on the architecture of Catholic church buildings during this period, both in Ireland and in Britain. However, the architecture of Rome continued to exercise influence, notably through the work of the architect J.J. McCarthy. St Michael's in Tipperary Town, consecrated in 1861, exemplifies his particular style

(fig. 160)
HOLY TRINITY CHURCH
Main Street,
Fethard
(1818-19)

Described as a 'full-blooded classical barn-church', the Catholic parish church at Fethard has an unusual, fanciful top to its pedimented gable-front.

(fig. 161)
HOLY TRINITY CHURCH

This most unusual example of Celtic Revival stained glass features Celtic interlace inspired by early Irish manuscripts. The lettering under the scene, in Gaelic script, reads 'I will sing unto thee among the nations'.

(fig. 162)
ST JOHN THE BAPTIST CHURCH
Friar Street,
Cashel
(1772-1804,
refronted c. 1890)

Cashel's Catholic parish church was built on the site of the town's long-destroyed medieval Franciscan friary. The building, designed by John Roberts, was built in 1772-1804; its present frontage and tower were added by W.G. Doolin c. 1890. The notable ashlar limestone gate piers have carved friezes and domed caps.

(fig. 163)
ST JOHN THE BAPTIST CHURCH

A dramatic interior is dominated by the unusual two-tier galleries running the length of the nave, the upper tier supported by classical columns and the lower by piers with colourful religious statuary and Stations of the Cross with carved timber frames having classical details.

(figs. 164-5). The building programme for this church was affected by the collapse of Sadlier's Bank, and as a result, the spire is more modest than intended. George Ashlin added the front

(fig. 164)
ST MICHAEL'S CHURCH
St Michael's Street, Tipperary
(1855-60)

St Michael's Church is regarded as one of the finest works of the renowned church architect, J.J. McCarthy, 'the Irish Pugin'. The builder was Philip McAuliffe, and George Ashlin designed the porch and a mortuary extension, both erected in 1915-16. The porch hides the fine original order arch doorway.

(fig. 165)
ST MICHAEL'S CHURCH

Detail of the magnificent reredos, the work of John Hardman. It was noted, at the time of its installation, as the largest reredos erected in Ireland or Britain since the Reformation.

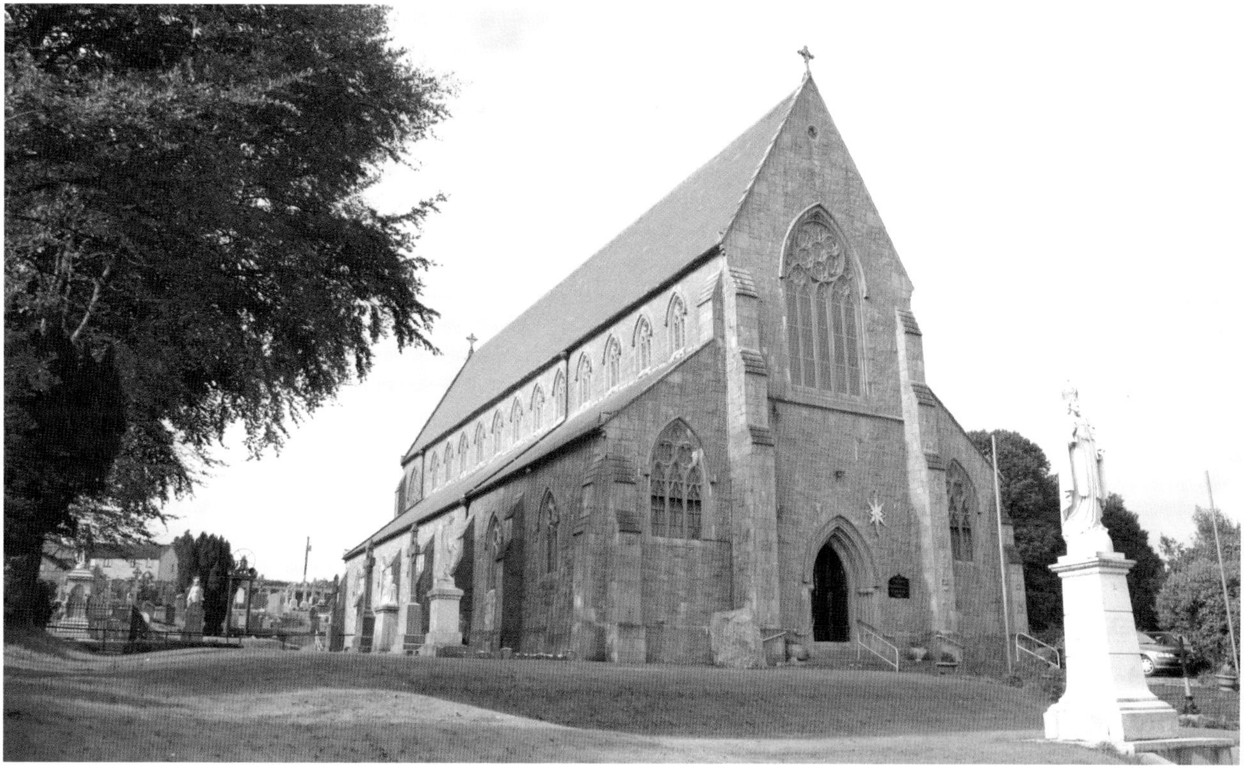

(fig. 166)
ST MARY'S CHURCH
Bailey Street,
Killenaule
(1859-65)

St Mary's was designed by the great church architect, J.J. McCarthy. It is sited in a commanding position in the town of Killenaule.

(fig. 167)
ST MARY'S CHURCH

The interior has a very fine colonnade, leading the eye towards the sumptuous reredos, installed in 1890, under one of the largest stained-glass windows in Ireland.

porch and mortuary chapel in the 1920s. St Mary's at Killenaule is an example of one of his smaller projects ***(figs. 166-7)***. St Patrick's Cemetery, Clonmel, established in 1886, is unusual for having Church of Ireland and

Roman Catholic chapels, both in the Gothic Revival style, a sexton's house in Tudor Revival style with fine terracotta dragon finials, and a fine set of entrance gates ***(figs.168-70)***.

(fig. 168)
ST PATRICK'S CEMETERY
Waterford Road,
Clonmel
(1886)

Clonmel's main cemetery has an unusual ensemble of Tudor Revival sexton's house and two Gothic Revival mortuary chapels, one Catholic and the other Church of Ireland, together with fine boundary walls and gates.

(fig. 169)
ST PATRICK'S CEMETERY

The sexton's house. The roof has terracotta dragon finials.

ST PATRICK'S CEMETERY

Detail of a dragon finial to the front gable of the sexton's house.

(fig. 170)
ST PATRICK'S CEMETERY

The Church of Ireland chapel.

The revival of Catholic political and economic influence is also visible in the building of convents, often on prominent sites, on the urban periphery. Some convents had been built in the eighteenth century, but after Catholic Emancipation there was a notable increase in the number and size of these developments. The complexes included chapels, gardens and, on occasion, industrial schools. St Anne's Convent in Tipperary Town opened in 1868, although the present building dates from 1877. The convent chapel was designed by George Ashlin and opened in 1885 ***(fig. 171)***). The fine Presentation Convent at Fethard is a particularly good example of a medium-sized convent building, dating from 1862, but having additions of 1885 ***(fig. 172)***). Rockwell College, near New Inn, is an impressive complex with its origins in a country house of c. 1830 ***(fig. 173)***.

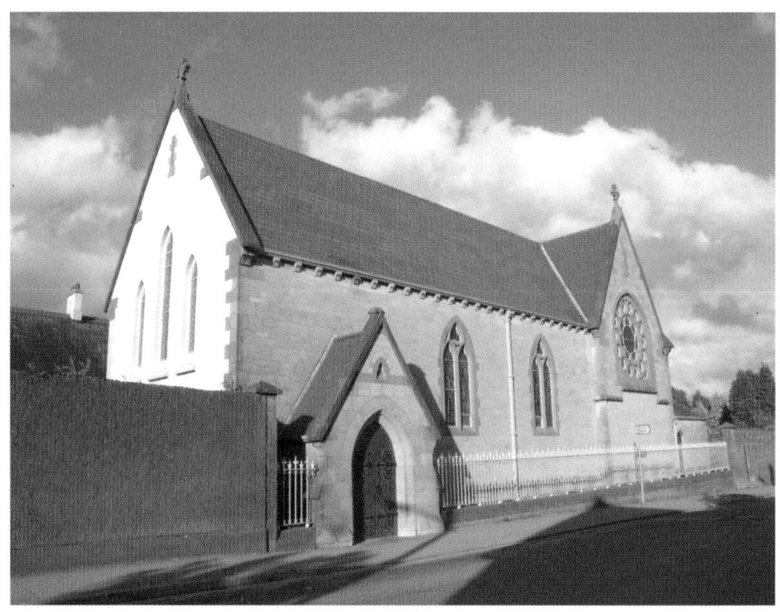

(fig. 171)
ST ANNE'S CONVENT
Rosanna Road,
Tipperary
(1886)

This convent chapel has high quality limestone work to its public façade, highlighted by the intricate rose window.

(fig. 172)
PRESENTATION CONVENT
Convent Lane,
Fethard
(1870-85)

The relatively modest convent of 1870 at Fethard was designed by Pugin and Ashlin, the projecting blocks, including the chapel being added in 1885.

(fig. 173)
ROCKWELL COLLEGE
Rockwell
(c. 1830-c. 1940)

The extensive buildings at Rockwell College, near New Inn, are centred on a former country house of c. 1830, whose interiors were Gothicised by William Tinsley in 1845. The Holy Ghost fathers set up a junior seminary in 1864. They commissioned George Ashlin c. 1895 to add the monastic-style ranges, campanile and St Patrick's Chapel. Other buildings and the entrance gates date to c. 1940. There are landscaped grounds with a boating lake.

(fig. 174)
KICKHAM MONUMENT
Kickham Street/
Main Street,
Tipperary
(1898)

South Tipperary's finest public monument is that to Charles J. Kickham (1828-82), writer and patriot. Designed by John Hughes, it stands in the middle of Tipperary Town and was unveiled in 1898. It features an elderly, seated Kickham with paper and quill.

Given the variations in economic circumstances, social and civic developments, the advent of improved communications and the defeat of landlordism, it is notable that the county's economy remained strongly agricultural and that, despite the impact of the Great Famine and the agrarian unrest, agricultural production increased rather than declined. The Land Acts had an impact on the size of smallholdings, but the strong farmer continued to be the backbone of the farming structure in South Tipperary. The pattern emerged of the family farm based on mixed tillage and livestock. However, the political landscape had been transformed, and the transition to the twentieth century was to see further bitter struggles before a new stability could be established ***(fig. 174)***.

(fig. 175)
WATERFORD ROAD
Carrick-on-Suir
(c. 1890)

This unusual colonial-style house is highly visible at the south end of Dillon Bridge. Its veranda, small-paned timber casement windows and the delicate valences to its eaves also give the building something of an Arts and Crafts appearance. The builder was reputedly a former sea captain on the China routes.

(fig. 176)
BALLYBRADA HOUSE
Ballybrada
(c. 1880)

This gate lodge near Cahir has an Arts and Crafts style, exemplified by the variously-sized windows and the range of decorative details.

The architecture of the county also shows the interplay between continuity and change. An interest in Gothic and Tudor Revival styles, and later the influence of the Arts and Crafts movement, can be clearly seen, often in the smaller houses and gate lodges ***(figs. 175-6)***. The influence of classicism was never quite lost and farmhouses built late in the century remain the distant but recognisable cousins of their eighteenth-century antecedents ***(figs. 177-8)***.

(fig. 177)
BALLYCREHANE HOUSE
Ballycrehane
(c. 1860)

The two-over-two pane sliding sash windows of this house at Lisvarrinane are typical of the second half of the nineteenth century. A high degree of symmetry is achieved by the three-bay plan and the centrally-placed chimneystacks.

(fig. 178)
FRIARSFIELD HOUSE
Friarsfield
(c. 1870)

Friarsfield House, near Tipperary Town, is an irregular-plan building, the tripartite ground floor windows of its façade having cut sandstone surrounds.

The Twentieth Century

(fig. 179)
BOER WAR MEMORIAL
Kickham Barracks,
Davis Road,
Clonmel
(1910)

Art Nouveau monuments are rare in Ireland. This example with a bronze figure, designed by R.C. Orpen, commemorates soldiers of the Royal Irish Regiment who died in South Africa during the Boer War. The pair of yew trees, representing immortality, provides a fitting backdrop.

The twentieth century opened with the anticipation of change. While economic circumstances were constrained, there was an expectation that the advances of previous decades would continue. However, the traumatic events of the Boer War (1899-1902), Great War (1914-18), the War of Independence (1918-21) and the Civil War (1922-3) brought political and social transformation on a scale few could have anticipated ***(figs. 179-81)***. The unrest that characterised the nineteenth century continued into the twentieth. Throughout the early years of the century, South Tipperary exhibited a high level of social radicalism and political militancy that found expression in the struggle for independence and in the Civil War. South Tipperary had a tradition of agrarian agitation going back two centuries, and a more recent history of social activism in the industrial sector. The Land Acts certainly benefited farmers, but as a whole, the population of County Tipperary declined, with the urban

(fig. 180)
WAR MEMORIAL
Castle Street,
Cahir
(1930)

Cahir's First World War dead are commemorated in the fine and well-maintained monument prominently sited near the castle.

WAR MEMORIAL

Detail of an inscribed panel listing soldiers who fell in the First World War.

(fig. 181)
LIAM LYNCH MEMORIAL
Crohan
(1935)

Liam Lynch died on 10th April 1923, during the Civil War. This memorial, in the style of early Christian round towers, was designed by Denis Doyle of Clonmel and the cast-bronze wolfhounds at the base are by Albert Power. The use of such symbols was intended to link the fallen leader with ancient heroes such as Cúchulainn. The tower stands on the northern slopes of the Knockmealdown Mountains, south of Newcastle.

(fig. 182)
TIPPERARY CO-OP
Station Road,
Tipperary
(1909)

The former Cleeves creamery at Tipperary was once completely clad in corrugated iron. Today only the east gable and projecting entrance block remain in the material. The cast-iron cresting, finial and timber casement windows are all typical details associated with corrugated-iron structures. The large Diocletian-style window is quite unexpected.

areas least affected. Tipperary Town even experienced a slight increase in population and by 1914 it had no fewer than three creameries, the largest of them employing 300 people, of whom a large proportion was female. The industrialisation of agriculture is well expressed in the creamery building for the co-operative society opened in 1909 in the same town and in continuous use since ***(fig. 182)***. It has corrugated-iron cladding in a refined utilitarian style and with good detailing, including a large Dicoletian-style window and decorative cresting. St Ailbe's Co-operative Creamery, Emly (c.1905), is a pleasant stone building at the heart of the Golden Vale dairying belt ***(fig. 183)***.

The young Free State found itself embroiled in the Economic War with Britain, which had a particularly damaging impact on areas that depended heavily on agricultural produce for their economic stability. The collapse in cattle prices led to the sale of farms and the weakening of the family farm structure that had provided the backbone of the rural economy. One of the defining characteristics of the years since 1922 has been the role of the State. From its early involvement in housing and education, to its promotion of electrification and industrial development, the first three quarters of the century bore witness to the crucial role of State bodies in creating the social and environmental

infrastructure of the emerging political entity. The final quarter of the century saw a further revolution in the management of the land, reflecting the impact of European Union policies on agriculture.

The county's stock of country houses suffered significantly during the War of Independence and Civil War. In the sixteen months from January 1922 to April 1923, twenty-nine were burned in the county, north and south. Several houses, such as Rochestown, near Cahir, Graiguenoe, near Holycross and Thomastown Castle, near Clogheen, were abandoned and fell into ruin. A smaller number, including Marlfield House and Tullamain Castle, were reconstructed. The loss of some other fine houses was, however, due to a combination of economic circumstance, antipathy and neglect.

The first half of the twentieth century has been characterised as one of general economic stagnation. Nonetheless, there was significant building activity, both by private individuals and by public bodies. In the public sector, much of the activity was devoted to the provision of housing, health, educational and other facilities, with a clear commitment to modernist expression in public buildings. But the early years of the century also saw a continuation in popularity of the use of stylistic

(fig. 183)
ST AILBE'S CREAMERY
Tulla (Emly par.)
(c. 1905)

Emly's creamery is distinguished by its two-pile plan. It is single-storey to the front and two-storey to the rear, and the concrete platform, which facilitated loading operations, incorporates a weighbridge.

(fig. 184)
CLONMEL POST OFFICE
(former)
Gladstone Street,
Clonmel
(1901)

Executed in Flemish Revival style by Edward Kavanagh, this former post office displays an accomplished use of brick, with many fine details in its pleasant, harmonious facade. The incorporation of a clock and a date plaque is typical of such public buildings. It was one of a series of post offices built in the county in the very early 1900s.

(fig. 185)
ST MICHAEL'S ROAD/MURGASTY
Tipperary
(c. 1900)

The veranda of this colonial-style bungalow in Tipperary is formed by fluted cast-iron columns supporting an ornate cast-iron valence.

elements of the Arts and Crafts idiom. The former post office building (1901), in Clonmel, and the current post office in Cahir, built a year later, both designed by the Office of Public Works, retain much of their original fabric and are attractive, well-designed examples of the style ***(fig. 184)***. The county has good examples of domestic buildings also. The semi-detached houses on the Mitchelstown Road in Cahir, built of sandstone, are intact examples of refined domestic building from the early years of the century. A house at Tipperary, built c. 1900, in a bungalow style, has an attractive veranda and good cast-iron detailing ***(fig. 185)***. At a more modest scale is the terraced house (1933) in Fethard that is well designed with detailing of the period still intact. The terrace was built 'through the beneficence of the late Misses M. and C. Mockler, Fethard' ***(fig. 186)***.

(fig. 186)
THE VALLEY
Fethard
(1933)

This modest house, in a terrace of similar houses erected 'through the benifi-cence of the late Misses M. & C. Mockler Fethard', has retained all of its external features and setting.

More classical in style is the courthouse at Cashel and the former National Bank in Clonmel ***(figs. 187-8)***. Quinlan's public house at Cullen has classical detailing, unusual for a small village ***(fig. 189)***. D.W. Parke's chemist shop in Clonmel (c. 1910) has exuberant Edwardian detailing ***(fig. 190).***

(fig. 188)
AIB BANK
65-67 O'Connell Street,
Clonmel
(c. 1935)

Built unusually late in the history of stone-fronted banks, this example stands out on Clonmel's principal thoroughfare due to its bulky form, ashlar limestone and the Giant Order engaged columns to its upper floors.

(fig. 187)
CASHEL COURTHOUSE
Hogan Square,
Cashel
(c.1910)

Cashel's relatively modest courthouse was provided with classical-style detailing to its principal elevation.

(fig. 189)
QUINLAN'S BAR
Cloonmanagh
(c. 1915)

Originally a plain building, this public house in the village of Cullen has been rendered with a host of ornate details and fine raised lettering.

(fig. 190)
D.W. PARKE
23 Gladstone Street,
Clonmel
(c. 1910)

This superb double-fronted Edwardian shopfront is unique in the county and has gold-leaf decoration under the glass-covered fascia. It was inserted into a terraced town house of c. 1840.

(fig. 191)
CASHEL POST OFFICE
Main Street/
Hogan Square,
Cashel
(1934)

Cashel's post office has a distinctive tower to its corner and combines classical references and Modernism.

However, the attitude of the young Free State held out a different promise for public architecture. In 1922, Darrell Figgis, then a minister in the government, called for 'simplicity and truth', the abandonment of 'antique manners' and the 'cleansing' of imitations, in what was akin to a manifesto for International Modernism. The 1930s witnessed a programme of modern construction to meet the requirements of the newly established Electricity Supply Board, and for the health and postal services. Cashel Post Office (1934) is an idiosyncratic combination of modern and traditional idioms ***(fig. 191)***. Its two-storey flat-roofed corner tower is almost abstract in its use of solid and void, but its single-storey elevations, to two streets, have strong historical references in the form of round-headed windows and, on one elevation, a pitched roof. Prior to the launch of a programme of hospital construction, the architect Vincent Kelly was commissioned by the government to study contemporary hospitals in a range of European countries. Kelly designed Our Lady's Hospital, Cashel, opened in 1940, as part of that programme. The massing, fenestration and the use of reinforced concrete, make this hospital a significant expression of the new architecture ***(fig. 191)***.

(fig. 192)
OUR LADY'S HOSPITAL
The Green,
Cashel
(1934-40)

Vincent Kelly designed this hospital, perhaps the finest Modern Movement building in South Tipperary, which opened in 1940.

The building has a fine main staircase. A newspaper at the time reported it as having '64 beds, with private wards for paying patients, is equipped in the most modern manner, and has an 'iron lung' provided by Lord Nuffield'.

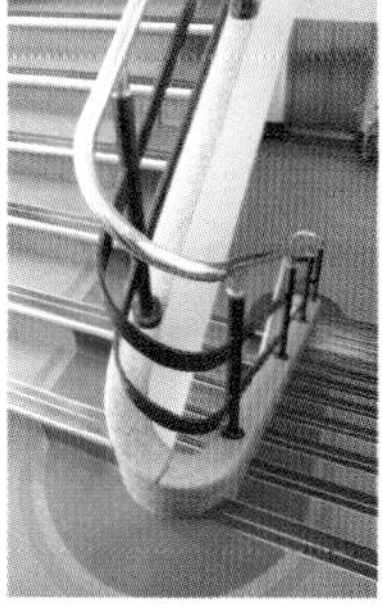

OUR LADY'S HOSPITAL

(fig. 193)
KILVEMNON NATIONAL SCHOOL
Kilvemnon
(1961)

Standard designs were produced for national schools throughout the State. This type has clerestory windows to the main block, projecting service wings to the front, a water tower to one end and a bicycle shed to the rear. The school is set in pleasantly lawned grounds.

(fig. 194)
SOUTH TIPPERARY ARTS CENTRE
Nelson Street,
Clonmel
(c. 1940)

Eoin Buckley was responsible for this former bus station in Clonmel. A modest, but representative example of the Modern Movement, it displays typical details of the style such as the flat roof, concrete canopy and the ribbon glazing.

The State, through the Office of Public Works, had instituted a building programme for schools from the late nineteenth century. In the decades after Independence, it was responsible for the construction of national schools and vocational schools in a simple modern style ***(fig. 192)***. The school complexes at Cahir (c.1930) and Cappawhite (c.1935) are attractive representatives of the building type and the Christian Brothers National School, Cashel (1937) is a good example of a large school of the time.

Distinguished small-scale examples of modernism were built throughout the county. The former bus terminus in Clonmel, designed by Eoin Buckley and dating from the late 1930s or early 1940s, is a fine if modest example ***(fig. 193)***. This architect worked for Michael Scott, who described it as a 'nice little building'. Other modernist buildings survive, though altered over time. Slattery's on Gladstone Street, Clonmel (c.1940), still retains its canopy, and its ribbon windows to the upper floors. Unfortunately, some other notable buildings have been lost to later development. Michael Scott modified the former RIC barracks on Parnell Street to create the Ritz Cinema. Now demolished, this was one of three cinemas designed by Scott, the others being in Athlone and Carlow.

A combination of low investment and the rise of private road transportation reduced the social and economic role of the rail network nationally, so that the mid-twentieth century witnessed the substantial undoing of the rail infrastructure created in the previous century. The last piece of South Tipperary's railway network to be built was the short branch-line connecting Clonmel with Thurles, which provided

Clonmel with a direct rail link to Dublin. The line succumbed to the cutbacks of the 1960s, passenger services ceased in 1969, and the track was dismantled in the 1980s. However, all of the small stations and most of the fine cut-stone bridges on the line survive. The stations at Fethard and Farranaleen are now domestic houses, but elsewhere, abandoned stationhouses and sheds remain as poignant reminders of the ambition of an earlier time. Some road bridges were constructed in the early part of the century, usually of reinforced concrete ***(fig. 195)***.

(fig. 195)
RITZ CINEMA
Parnell Street/College Street
Clonmel
(c.1940)

Michael Scott modified the former RIC barracks on Parnell Street to create the Ritz Cinema, one of three cinemas designed by him, now all demolished. This contemporary drawing highlights the modernist overcoat: a large window shaded by teak laths over the entrance canopy, a tower clad in a grid of teak that allowed the interior lighting to flood into the street at night, and a vertical panel displaying the name of the cinema.

(fig. 196)
CAPPA NEW BRIDGE
Tankerstown/
Cappauniac
(Clonbullogue par.)
(1934)

Good use of concrete is evident in this bridge across the Aherlow River, near Cahir. Arched pedestrian ways at each of the four corners give access to the river bank.

(fig. 197)
ST MICHAEL'S CHURCH
Callan Street,
Mullinahone
(1969)

This is a rare example of a full-blooded modernist church in South Tipperary.

Traditional approaches dominated church architecture well into the century, with buildings designed in styles that would be appropriate to the nineteenth century appearing as late as the 1960s. The exterior of the Church of Our Lady of the Assumption at Burncourt is traditional, but the portal frames inside are ruggedly modernist. St Michael's Roman Catholic Church in Mullinahone is more full-blooded ***(fig. 196)***. Cruciform in plan, it was built in 1969 with a low-pitched roof over a continuous clerestory. Its entrance canopy links it to a belfry tower in a successful composition. A similar approach is evident in schools of the same period.

The years following the Second World War brought a renewed interest in planning for the future. The First Programme for Economic Expansion was launched in 1958 and set out targets for economic and agricultural development. The Local Government (Planning and Development) Act of 1963 established a system of physical planning that has attempted to control the development pressures of alternate waves of economic expansion and recession. The survival, until the 1960s, of much of the architectural heritage of South Tipperary, can be attributed, at least in part, to the relatively low level of prosperity and economic growth. However, since then both town and countryside have experienced the forces of change.

(fig. 198)
CASTLEJOHN
(c. 1900-40)

A conveniently sited water pump and letter box at a crossroads at Castlejohn, near Ahenny.

Conclusion

The architecture of South Tipperary bears witness to a continuity of settlement from the medieval period into modern times. Its legacy of buildings from the medieval period through to the twentieth centuries, while sharing characteristics common to buildings elsewhere in the country, is distinctive and memorable. The urban structure of the county has remained relatively intact for hundreds of years, while the landscape still bears the imprint of traditional landholding patterns.

In recent years development pressures have put the future of the more modest buildings of the past under threat, as the value of sites for their development potential has become ever more apparent. The planning system has struggled to reconcile the need to build within existing urban environments to reduce urban sprawl with the need to protect older buildings and streetscapes of value. The struggle has often been a hard one, despite the advent of greatly improved legislation at the turn of the twenty-first century.

The later years of the twentieth century saw a renewed interest in good modern architecture in Ireland and some new buildings have attracted international interest. As in other countries, increased awareness of the importance of the buildings of the past has resulted in the conservation of a number of buildings in South Tipperary that are of national and international importance. This conservation effort has been conducted almost exclusively by the State, under the National Monuments Acts. Works at the Rock of Cashel, for example, have been a feature of its involvement since it became responsible for this iconic site in the mid-nineteenth century. Work on the cathedral and on Cormac's Chapel, where the beautiful medieval wall-paintings are among the finest of those few surviving in Ireland, continues to reveal aspects of medieval art that had been lost for centuries. Ormond Castle at Carrick-on-Suir, and Cahir Castle have also gained from several campaigns of conservation. The Main Guard at Clonmel is a building whose transformations have mirrored the social and political history of South Tipperary. It has now been conserved and its reinstated arcade restores a historic urban space in the town that had been lost in the building frenzy of the early nineteenth century. Also in Clonmel, Richard Morrison's courthouse has been restored and continues to serve its original judicial function.

Apart from the notable examples of State-led conservation in the towns, some communities, in rural as well as urban areas, have sought to repair their older secular or religious buildings and bring them back into useful life. The many hundreds of historic houses and other buildings and features around the county need careful stewardship to ensure their continuing survival and in this regard it would be most appropriate that South Tipperary County Council take the lead and guide this conservation effort.

However, new architectural challenges have also emerged. Contemporary buildings must provide for access to people of all abilities, as well as to demands for increased energy efficiency. The increasing importance of sustainable development will undoubtedly leave its mark on the new buildings we bequeath to future generations.

PLAIN OF CASHEL
Looking from The Vee.
The Galtee Mountains are
on the left.

Further Reading

Bassett, George Henry
County Tipperary One Hundred Years Ago
(Belfast: Friar's Bush Press, 1991; originally published as The Book of County Tipperary, Dublin, 1889)

Bence-Jones, Mark,
A Guide to Irish Country Houses
(London: Constable Press, 1988)

Butler, David J,
The churches and church plate of the Church of Ireland in the dioceses of Cashel, Emly, Waterford and Lismore'
Journal of the Royal Society of Antiquaries of Ireland
(Vol. 134 (2004) 91-165)

Craig, Maurice,
Classic Irish Houses of the Middle Size
(London: Architectural Press, 1976)

Craig, Maurice,
The Architecture of Ireland from the Earliest Times to 1880
(London: Batsford and Dublin: Eason, 1989)

Craig, Maurice and Garner, William
National Heritage Inventory: Buildings of Architectural, historic and artistic interest in County Tipperary: South Riding
(Dublin: An Foras Forbartha, 1975, unpublished)
Craig, Maurice and Knight of Glin
Ireland Observed: a guide to the buildings and antiquities of Ireland
(Dublin and Cork: Mercier Press, 1970)

Danaher, Kevin
Ireland's Traditional Houses
(Dublin: Bord Fáilte Mercier Press, 1991)

Dunne, Mildred and Phillips, Brian
The Courthouses of Ireland: a gazetteer of Irish courthouses
(Kilkenny: The Heritage Council, 1999)

Glin, The Knight of, Griffin, David J. and Robinson, Nicholas K.,
Vanishing Country Houses of Ireland
(Dublin: The Irish Architectural Archive and The Irish Georgian Society, 1988)

Hutchison, Sam
Towers, Spires and Pinnacles: a history of the cathedrals and churches of the Church of Ireland
(Bray: Wordwell, 2003)

Johnson, Stephen,
Johnson's Atlas and Gazetteer of the Railways of Ireland
(Leicester: Midland Publishing Ltd, 1997)

Killanin, Lord and Duignan, Michael V.,
The Shell Guide to Ireland
(London: Ebury Press, 1962)

Lewis, Samuel
A Topographical Dictionary of Ireland Volumes I and II
(London: Samuel Lewis and Company, 1837)

McParland, Edward,
Public Architecture in Ireland 1680-1760
(New Haven and London: Yale University Press, 2001)

Nolan, William and McGrath, Thomas, G. (eds)
Tipperary: History and Society
(Dublin: Geography Publications, 1985)

O'Keeffe, Peter and Simington, Tom
Irish Stone Bridges: history and heritage
(Dublin: Irish Academic Press, 1991)
Shaffrey, Patrick and Maura,
Buildings of Irish Towns: Treasures of Everyday Architecture
(Dublin: The O'Brien Press, 1983)

Shaffrey, Patrick and Maura,
Irish Countryside Buildings: Everyday Architecture in the Rural Landscape
(Dublin: The O'Brien Press, 1985)

Shee, Elizabeth and Watson, S.J.
Clonmel: an architectural guide.
(Dublin: An Taisce, 1975)

Williams, Jeremy,
A Companion Guide to the Architecture of Ireland 1837-1921
(Dublin: Irish Academic Press, 1994)

KILLOUGH CASTLE

Registration Numbers

The structures mentioned in the text of this Introduction are listed below. It is possible to find more information on each structure by accessing our Inventory on the Internet at: ***www.buildingsofireland.ie*** *and searching by the Registration Number, structure name, or location. The structures below are listed by page number. Please note that the majority of the structures included in this book are privately owned and not open to the public. However, ecclesiastical buildings such as churches, commercial buildings such as shops, public houses, banks and railway stations in use, are normally accessible. Courthouses and some other buildings have variable access. Other buildings, such as hotels, are normally accessible and are asterisked.*

05 (Golden Bridge) Baurstookeen/Castlepark/Persses -Lot/Hoops'-Lot, Golden
Reg. 22104010

06-07 Cormac's Chapel*, St Patrick's Rock, Cashel
Not included in survey

06-07 Derrynaflan Island*, Lurgoe Td.
Not included in survey

08-09 Athassel Abbey*, Athasselabbey North Td.
Not included in survey

10 Lisronagh/Shanbally (Lisronagh ED) Tds.
Not included in survey

11 Cahir Castle*, Castle Street, Cahir
Not included in survey

12 Watergate Street, Fethard
Reg. 22110046

12 Killenure Castle
Not included in survey

12-14 Fethard Town Hall, Main Street, Fethard
Reg. 22110021

14-15 Main Guard*, Mitchell Street/ Sarsfield Street, Clonmel
Reg. 22117066

16 Meldrum House, Meldrum Td.
Reg. 22206104

17 Old Bridge, Carrick-on-Suir
Reg. 22123027

17 Sir Thomas's Bridge, Ferryhouse/Twomilebridge Tds.
Reg. 22208321

19 Marlfield House*, Marlfield
Reg. 22112003

20 Marlfield House gates, Marlfield
Reg. 22112012

20-21 Knocklofty House*, Knocklofty Demesne Td.
Reg. 22208216

21 Knocklofty House gates, Knocklofty Demesne Td.
Reg. 22208211

21 Knocklofty House, gate lodge, Knocklofty Demesne Td.
Reg. 22208212

18,22 Ardfinnan Castle, Ardfinnan
Reg. 22126001

22 Thomastown Castle, Thomastown Castle Demesne Td.
Reg. 22206025

22-23 Kiltinan Castle, Kiltinan Td.
Reg. 22207019

23 Kiltinan Castle gates, Kiltinan Td.
Reg. 22207022

22-23 Barne Park, Barn Demesne Td.
Reg. 22207612

24-25 Cashel Palace Hotel*, Main Street, Cashel
Reg. 22105030

25 Cashel Palace Hotel gate lodge, Main Street, Cashel
Reg. 22105032

24-25 Dundrum House*, Dundrum
Reg. 22102010

26-27 Clonbrogan House, Clonbrogan Td.
Reg. 22206203

27 Manganstown House, Mauganstown Td.
Reg. 22207814

27 Corrabella House, Corrabella Td.
Reg. 22208806

28 John Christian House, New Quay, Clonmel
Reg. 22117087

28 Friar Street, Carrick-on-Suir
Reg. 22123028

28 Salisbury, Salisbury Td.
Reg. 22201204

29 Killough Castle, Killough Td.
Reg. 22204707

29 The Glebe, Templenoe Td.
Reg. 22205910

29 Shanrahan graveyard, Shanrahan Td.
Reg. 221250

29 22 Gladstone Street, Clonmel
Reg. 22117020

30-31 Ballyowen House, Newpark Td.
Reg. 22205316

31,59 Longfield House, Longfield Td.
Reg. 22205209

31-32 Anne's Gift, Annesgift Td.
Reg. 22206216

32 Millgrove House, Tincurry Td.
Reg. 22208112

32 Ballingarrane House, Ballingarrane Td.
Reg. 22208307

32-33 Glenconnor House, Glenconnor Td.
Reg. 22208309

33 The Guggy, Knocklofty Demesne Td.
Reg. 22208215

34 Newcastle Bridge, Moloughnewtown/Clashganny West Tds.
Reg. 22208811

34-35 Fethard Rectory, Fethard
Reg. 22110001

35 Former parochial house, Main Street, Fethard
Reg. 22110008

35 O'Shea's, Burke Street, Fethard
Reg. 22110032

35 Abymill Theatre, Abbeyville, Fethard
Reg. 22110039

35-37 Cathedral of St John the Baptist and St Patrick's Rock, John Street, Cashel
Reg. 22105077

38 Castlegrace Mill, Castlegrace Td.
Reg. 22208711

39 Main Guard, Mitchell Street/Sarsfield Street, Clonmel
Reg. 22117066

39 Gaol, Emmet Street, Clonmel
Reg. 22117027

39 Abbey Grammar School, Abbey Street/Station Road, Tipperary
Reg. 22108101

39-40 Silverspring House, St Patrick's Road, Clonmel
Reg. 22115002

39-41 Cashel Charter School, Charter-School Land, Cashel
Not included in survey

40,42 St Mary's Church of Ireland Church, Mary Street, Clonmel
Reg. 22117013

40, 42,43 Holy Trinity Church of Ireland Church, Main Street, Fethard
Reg. 22110022

41 Glebe House, Kilvemnon Td.
Reg. 22206315

42,44 St Mary's Church, Bansha
Reg. 22109008

45 Tullaghmelan Church of Ireland, Ballybeg (Tullaghmelan par.) Td.
Reg. 22208801

45 Lismalin Church of Ireland, Lismalin Td.
Reg. 22205521

46 Moanvurrin Td.
Reg. 22206302

46 Ballylynch Td.
Reg. 22208506

47 Bothán Scóir, Clonmel Road, Cashel
Reg. 22105084

48 Hearn's Hotel, Parnell Street, Clonmel
Reg. 22117046

49 Ardfinnan Bridge, Ardfinnan
Reg. 22126003

49 Wilford Bridge, Shangarry Td.
Reg. 22205515

49 Kingston Bridge, Barnahown Td.
Reg. 22208902

50-51 Clonmel Railway Station, Thomas Street, Clonmel
Reg. 22113001-3

50 Tipperary Railway Station, Station Road, Tipperary
Reg. 22108102

50 Dundrum Railway Station, Gortarush Upper Td.
Reg. 22205113

50,129 Fethard Railway Station, Cashel Road, Fethard
Reg. 22110003

50 Goold's Cross Railway Station, Clonoulty Churchquarter Td.
Reg. 22205205

52,129 Farranaleen Railway Station, Farranaleen Td.
Reg. 22206210

52 Kennedy's Bar, Clonoulty Churchquarter
Reg. 22205207

53 Cahir Railway Station, Church Street, Cahir
Reg. 22111017

53 Suir Bridge, Caherabbey Upper/ Townparks (Caher par.), Cahir
Reg. 22111011

54-55 Mardyke Td.
Reg. 22205403

54 Knockalonga Td.
Reg. 22204910

54-55 The War House*, Farranrory Upper Td.
Reg. 22204909

55 The Steeple of Copper, Ballingarry Lower Td.
Reg. 22205502

56-57 Kiltinan Td.
Reg. 22207018

57 Ballylusky Td (Magowry par.) Td.
Reg. 22206206

58 The Swiss Cottage*, Kilcommon More (North) Td.
Reg. 22208107

58-59 Shanbally Castle, Shanbally Demesne Td.
Not included in survey

59 Bianconi Mortuary Chapel, Ardmayle East Td.
Reg. 22205305

60 Coolville House, Lower Main Street, Clogheen
Reg. 22125003

60-61 Newtownanner House, Newtownanner Demesne Td.
Reg. 22207718

61 The Temple Water, Newtownanner Demesne Td.
Reg. 22207722

60,62 Kilcooly Abbey, Kilcoolyabbey Td.
Reg. 22204309

60,62 Thomastown Castle, Thomastown Demesne Td.
Reg. 22206025

62 Tullamain Castle, Tullamain Td.
Reg. 22206906

62-63 Lismacue House, Lismacue Td.
Reg. 22109011

64-65 Lakefield, Ballygambon Td.
Reg. 22207016

64 Summerhill House, Summerhill Td.
Reg. 22208304

64 Sunville, Ardgeeha Lower/Burgagery-Lands West Tds.
Reg. 22208305

65 Grove House, Strike Upper Td.
Reg. 22207007

65 9 Emmet Street, Tipperary
Not included in survey.

65 O'Brien Arcade, Tipperary
Not included in survey.

66 Kilmurry Lodge, Ballynamona (Kilmurry par.) Td.
Reg. 22207813

66-67 Mountain Lodge, Cullenagh (Shanrahan par.) Td.
Reg. 22208001

67 Ballyduggan Td.
Reg. 22207103

67 Noan Td.
Reg. 22205311

68 Moorstown Td.
Reg. 22207611

68-69 Monslatt Td.
Reg. 22205406

69 Murgasty Td.
Reg. 22206701

70 Oldbridge, Clonmel
Not included in survey

70-71 Main Guard, Mitchell Street/Sarsfield Street, Clonmel
Reg. 22117066

70-71 West Gate, O'Connell Street/Irishtown, Clonmel
Reg. 22117052

71 Fethard Augustinian Abbey, Abbeyville, Fethard
Reg. 22110038

72 John Street, Cashel
Reg. 22105070

72-73 O'Connor Bros, 35-36 Main Street, Tipperary
Reg. 22108078

73 22-25 Gladstone Street, Clonmel
Reg. 22117017-20

75 M. Ryan, 76 Main Street, Cashel
Reg. 22105035

76 The Square, Cahir
Reg. 22111072-4

76 W.J. Irwin, The Square, Cahir
Reg. 22111074

77 Castle Street, Cahir
Reg. 22111042

78 The Auld Murray Inn, 7 Main Street, Tipperary
Reg. 22108082

79 Fitzgibbon, Main Street/Chapel Street, Cappawhite
Reg. 22101003

80 Government Offices, New Quay/Nelson Street, Clonmel
Reg. 22117091

80-81 Castlegrace Td.
Reg. 22208710

82 Clonmel Arms Hotel, Sarsfield Street, Clonmel
Reg. 22117073

82 AIB Bank, Lower Main Street, Clogheen
Reg. 22125007

83 Bank of Ireland, Parnell Street/Nelson Street, Clonmel
Reg. 22117070

83 Former Clanwilliam Club/Sadlier's Bank, Bank Place, Tipperary
Reg. 22108094

84-85 1-24 Anne Street, Clonmel
Reg. 22116005-22116028

84 9 Anne Street, Clonmel
Reg. 22116020

85 The Mall, Cahir
Reg. 22111037-40

85 3-4 New Quay, Clonmel
Reg. 22117089-90

85-86 1-10 Doctor Croke Place, Clonmel
Reg. 22117099-22117103; 22118002-22118006

86-87 Minella Hotel, Coleville Road, Clonmel
Reg. 22118011

87 Melview, Prior Park Road, Clonmel
Reg. 22113011

87 Loreto Convent, Coleville Road, Clonmel
Reg. 22122003

87 Ashbourne, Coleville Road, Clonmel
Reg. 22122002

88 Ahenny Td.
Reg. 22207902

88 Monksland Td.
Reg. 22208207-22208208

88-89 St Francis' Court, King Street, Clonmel
Reg. 22114001

89 Back of the Pipes, Main Street, Clonmel
Reg. 22105042

89 Butler Charteris Fountain, The Square, Cahir
Reg. 22111050

90 Clonoulty Churchquarter Td.
Reg. 22204612

90 Free School, Western Road, Clonmel
Reg. 22116030

90-91 Erasmus Smith Building*, Church Street, Cahir
Reg. 22111014

90-91 Model School, Western Road, Clonmel
Reg. 22116004

90,92 Abbey School, Abbey Street/Station Road, Tipperary
Reg. 22108101

92-93 Curraghpoor National School, Gorteen (Rathlynin par.) Td.
Reg. 22205905

90, 92-93 Abbey School, Abbey Street/Station Road, Tipperary
Reg. 22108101

93 Parish Pastoral Centre*, Friar Street, Cashel
Reg. 22105072

94 Clonmel Courthouse, Nelson Street, Clonmel
Reg. 22117083

94-95 Clonmel Town Hall, Parnell Street, Clonmel
Reg. 22117069

95 Cashel Tourist Office, Main Street, Cashel
Reg. 22105040

95 Former Cahir Town Hall*, The Square, Cahir
Reg. 22111047

95 Carrick-on-Suir Courthouse, Greenside South, Carrick-on-Suir
Reg. 22123007

95 Clogheen Courthouse, Barrack Hill, Clogheen
Reg. 22125015

96 Tipperary Courthouse, St Michael's Street, Tipperary
Reg. 22108017

96 Carrigeen Castle, Mitchelstown Road, Cahir
Reg. 22111025

96 Tipperary Bridewell, St Michael's Street, Tipperary
Reg. 22108018

97 Officers' Mess, Kickham Barracks, Davis Road, Clonmel
Reg. 22118020

97 Privates' Mess, Kickham Barracks, Clonmel
Reg. 22118018

97 Cahir Military Barracks, Kilcommon More (North) Td.
Reg. 22208104

97-98 Tipperary Military Barracks, Station Road, Tipperary
Reg. 22108105

98 Clonmel Garda Station, Emmet Street, Clonmel
Reg. 22117040

98 Tipperary RIC Barracks, Davis Street/St Michael's Road, Tipperary
Reg. 22108020

99 Dundrum Garda Station, Garryduff East Td., Dundrum
Reg. 22102004

99 Mealclye Td.
Reg. 22205111

100 Cashel Workhouse (now St Patrick's Hospital), Cahir Road, Cashel
Reg. 22105082

100 Tipperary Workhouse, Station Road, Tipperary
Reg. 22108107

100 South Tipperary General Hospital, Western Road, Clonmel
Reg. 22116001

100-1 St Luke's Hospital, Western Road, Clonmel
Reg. 22116002

102 St Patrick's Church, Marlfield
Reg. 22112014

102-3 St John's Church, Ardmayle
Reg. 22205217

102-3 Kilcooly Church, Kilcoolyabbey Td.
Reg. 22204308

102, 104 Killaloan Lower Td.
Reg. 22208319

102, 104 Magorban Church, Magorban Td.
Reg. 22206107

104, 106 St Mary's Church, Church Street, Tipperary
Reg. 22108041

104-5 St Paul's Church, Cahir
Reg. 22111019

106 Scots' Church, James Street/John Street, Tipperary
Reg. 22108049

106 White Memorial Theatre, Wolfe Tone Street, Clonmel
Reg. 22117036

106-7 Cahir Presbyterian Church, Abbey Street, Cahir
Reg. 22111010

106-7 Bolton Library*, John Street, Cashel
Reg. 22105078

108-9 St Mary's Catholic Church, Irishtown, Clonmel
Reg. 22116032

110 Holy Trinity Catholic Church, Main Street, Fethard
Reg. 22110009

110 Church of the Annunciation, Bansha West Td., Bansha
Reg. 22109009

110 St Mary's Catholic Church, Barrack Hill, Clogheen
Reg. 22125014

110 St Nicholas of Myra Catholic Church, Wiliam Street, Carrick-on-Suir
Reg. 22123010

111 St John the Baptist Catholic Church, Friar Street, Cashel
Reg. 22105075

112 St Michael's Church, St Michael's Street, Tipperary
Reg. 22108019

113 St Mary's Catholic Church, Bailey Street, Killenaule
Reg. 22103005

113-5 St Patrick's Cemetery, Waterford Road, Clonmel
Reg. 22115004-22115006

116 St Anne's Convent, Rosanna Road, Tipperary
Reg. 22108005

116 Presentation Convent, Convent Lane, Fethard
Reg. 22110007

116-7 Rockwell College, Rockwell Td.
Reg. 22206909

117 Kickham Monument, Kickham Street/Main Street, Tipperary
Reg. 22108086

118 Waterford Road, Carrick-on-Suir
Reg. 22123033

118 Ballybrada House, Ballybrada Td.
Reg. 22208114

119 Ballycrehane House, Ballycrehane Td.
Reg. 22207304

119 Friarsfield House, Friarsfield Td.
Reg. 22205916

120 Boer War Memorial, Kickham Barracks, Davis Road, Clonmel
Reg. 22117138

121 War Memorial, Castle Street, Cahir
Reg. 22111053

121 Liam Lynch Memorial, Crohan Td.
Reg. 22209101

122 Tipperary Co-Op, Station Road, Tipperary
Reg. 22108100

122-3 St Ailbe's Creamery, Tulla (Emly par.) Td., Emly
Reg. 22107007

124-5 Clonmel Post Office (former), Gladstone Street, Clonmel
Reg. 22117025

125 Cahir Post Office, Church Street, Cahir
Reg. 22111034

125 Mitchelstown Road, Cahir
Reg. 22111027-8

125 St Michael's Road/Murgasty, Tipperary
Reg. 22108009

125 The Valley, Fethard
Reg. 22110042

126 Cashel Courthouse, Hogan Square, Cashel
Reg. 22105019

126 AIB Bank, 65-67 O'Connell Street, Clonmel
Reg. 22117043

126 Quinlan's Bar, Cloonmanagh Td.
Reg. 22205804

127 Cashel Post Office, Main Street/Hogan Square, Cashel
Reg. 22105022

127 Our Lady's Hospital, The Green, Cashel
Reg. 22105081

128 Education Centre (former Vocational School), Church Street, Cahir
Reg. 22111021

128 An Ceárd Scoil, Cappawhite
Reg. 22101009

128 Cashel CBS, Golden Road, Cashel
Reg. 22105086

128 Kilvemnon National School, Kilvemnon Td.
Reg. 22206318

128 South Tipperary Arts Centre, Nelson Street, Clonmel
Reg. 22117078

128 Slattery's, Gladstone Street, Clonmel
Reg. 22117022

128-9 Ritz Cinema, Parnell Street/College Street, Parnell
Not included in survey

130 Cappa New Bridge, Tankerstown/Cappauniac (Clonbullogue par.)
Reg. 22207503

130-1 St Michael's Church, Callan Street, Mullinahone
Reg. 22106007

131 Our Lady of the Assumption, Burncourt
Reg. 22208601

131 Castlejohn Td.
Reg. 22207205

135 Killough Castle, Killough Td.
Reg. 22204707

139 Moatquarter Td.
Reg. 22205921

ST PATRICK'S CHURCH
Churchquarter, Kilfeakle

Detail of stained-glass window dedicated to St Aidan, depicted Rock of Cashel and St Dominic's Abbey.

Acknowledgements

NIAH

Senior Architect Willy Cumming
Survey Controller Barry O'Reilly
GIS Technicians Gareth John and Alan Murray
Additional NIAH Staff Mildred Dunne, Deborah Lawlor, Damian Murphy, Flora O'Mahony, T.J. O'Meara, Marc Ritchie, Ann Kennedy and Emer Mulhall

The NIAH gratefully acknowledges the following in the preparation of the South Tipperary Survey and Introduction:

Survey Fieldwork

Jane Wales Associates

Recorders

Jane Wales, Brigid Fitzgerald, Marie Anne Lennon, Sandra O'Brien, Jennifer O'Leary, Natalie de Róiste, Allyson Smyth

Introduction

Writers Margaret Quinlan, Loughlin Kealy
Editors Barry O'Reilly, Willy Cumming
Copy Editor Lucy Freeman
Photographer Shannon Images (Pádraig O'Reilly, Mary O'Reilly and Pádraic O'Reilly)
Designed by Bennis Design
Printed by Brunswick Press

The NIAH wishes to thank all of those who allowed access to their property for the purpose of the Architectural Inventory of South Tipperary and subsequent photography.

The NIAH gratefully acknowledges the following in the preparation of the Architectural Inventory of South Tipperary and the Introduction: Stephen Fallon and Sheila Butterly, Brendan McSherry, Captain Brady (Kickham Barracks), Liam Ó Duibhir, Joe Kenny, Dean Philip Knowles, Rev. Arthur Carter, Tom Wood, Bob Withers and Jean Farrelly.

The NIAH also wishes to acknowledge the generous assistance given by the staff of the Irish Architectural Archive, the National Library of Ireland, the National Photographic Archive; Mary Alice O'Connor, Excel Centre, Tipperary; Mary Guinan-Darmody and the staff of the Local Studies Department, Tipperary County Library; Hugh O'Brien, South Tipperary County Council; Con Brogan and the staff of the photographic unit, Department of the Environment, Heritage and Local Government; our archaeological colleagues in the Department of the Environment, Heritage and Local Government, particularly Jean Farrelly, Caimin O'Brien and Con Manning; Aighleann O'Shaughnessy, Office of Public Works.

Sources of Illustrations

Original photographs for the Introduction were taken by Pádraig O'Reilly, Mary O'Reilly and Pádraic O'Reilly, of Shannon Images. The illustrations listed below are identified by their figure or page number:

figs. 15, 16, fig. 26 (p. 24), 29, 34, 38, 51, 53, 58-60, 64-5, 68, 73-4, 77-8, 80, 87, 89, 93, 96, 102-3, 109 (bottom right), 110-11, 113, 121-2, 124, 128, 138, 146, 149, 151, 177-8, 181, 186 are the work of Jane Wales Associates; p. 3, fig. 7, p. 70 (top left), fig. 100, figs. 106-7, 119, 136-7, 139-41, 152, 171, 173, 179 are the work of the NIAH; figs. 23, 50, 79, 83, 84, 100, 131 are used courtesy of the Irish Architectural Archive; figs. 2-4, 6, 10 are reproduced courtesy of the photographic unit of the Department of Environment, Heritage and Local Government; figs. 90, p. 75, p. 79 are the property of the National Library of Ireland and have been reproduced with the permission of the Council of Trustees of the National Library of Ireland; figs. 21, 98 are used courtesy of Jean Farrelly; fig. 36 is used courtesy of Tom Ryan; fig. 5 is used courtesy of Barry O'Reilly.

The NIAH has made every effort to source and acknowledge the owners of all the archival illustrations included in this Introduction. The NIAH apologises for any omissions made, and would be happy to include such acknowledgements in future issues of the Introduction.

Please note that most of the structures included in the Architectural Inventory of South Tipperary are privately owned and are therefore not open to the public.

ISBN: 0-7557-7445-0